THE DEVELOPING CHILD

Recent decades have witnessed unprecedented advances in research on human development. In those same decades there have been profound changes in public policy toward children. Each book in the Developing Child series reflects the importance of such research in its own right and as it bears on the formulation of policy. It is the purpose of the series to make the findings of this research available to those who are responsible for raising a new generation and for shaping policy in its behalf. We hope that these books will provide rich and useful information for parents, educators, child-care professionals, students of developmental psychology, and all others concerned with the challenge of human growth.

Jerome Bruner
New York University

Michael Cole
University of California, San Diego

Annette Karmiloff-Smith
Medical Research Council, London

SERIES EDITORS

The Developing Child Series

The Child's Discovery of the Mind

Janet Wilde Astington

Harvard University Press
Cambridge, Massachusetts
1993

This book is printed on acid-free paper, and its binding materials
have been chosen for strength and durability.

Library of Congress Cataloging-in-Publication Data

Astington, Janet W.
  The child's discovery of the mind / Janet Wilde Astington
    p. cm.—(The Developing child)
  Includes bibliographical references and index.
  ISBN 0-674-11641-0 (alk. paper).—ISBN 0-674-11642-9 (pbk.: alk. paper)
  1. Philosophy of mind in children. 2. Cognition in children.
  I. Title.. II. Series.
BF723.P48A77 1993
155.4'13—dc20

93-4784
  CIP

In loving memory of my father, George Wilde, 1902–1991

Acknowledgments

This book was begun a long time ago. I was a botanist and a teacher, then I had two daughters. I can still remember my delight and amazement as they discovered the mind, although I did not call it that at the time. Watching them learn to talk and play together turned me from botany to psychology. I went to the Ontario Institute for Studies in Education, where I met David Olson and Robbie Case, who became my mentors, friends, and colleagues. I want to thank them for their generous contributions to my intellectual development, and to this book.

Soon after I graduated from OISE, Lynd Forguson, Alison Gopnik, David Olson, and I organized an international conference, "Developing Theories of Mind" at the University of Toronto. It was there that I first met many of the people whose work informs this book. Since then I have enjoyed a continuous exchange of papers and ideas within a lively community of theory-of-mind colleagues on both sides of the Atlantic. Many of them, and other friends and students, have read drafts of the book; their criticism, their encouragement, and their anecdotes make it what it is: I particularly thank Josef Perner, Paul Harris, Alison Gopnik, Henry Wellman, Sue Leekam, Simon Baron-Cohen, Daniela O'Neill, Joan Peskin, Jenny Jenkins, and John Astington.

I also thank everyone in my home institution, the Institute of Child Study in the University of Toronto's Faculty of Education, for their warm support—children and teachers, students, researchers, faculty, and support staff—and especially Carl Corter, Chair of the Institute, and Michael Fullan, Dean of the Faculty. I cannot think of a better place in which to study and write about children. And I would like to acknowledge the funding support that made this study and writing possible—from the Social Sciences and Humanities Research Council of Canada, the Natural Sciences and Engineering Research Council of Canada, and the National Academy of Education through a Spencer Postdoctoral Fellowship.

I also take this opportunity to thank Angela von der Lippe and Linda Howe, of Harvard University Press, for their guidance and patience. Finally, I am extremely grateful to Jerome Bruner, whose work I have long admired, for his encouragement and support.

Contents

The Child's
Discovery
of the Mind

1 / What Is the Mind?

- "I've changed my mind."
- "Have you made up your mind?"
- "His mind was wandering."

What are these minds that we all have? Why did I change mine? How do you make yours up? Where was his wandering to? What makes us think we have minds at all? Look about you. We can see bodies, at least their outer surface, and we know something of the existence of muscle, blood, bone, and nerves under the skin. We can see the body and watch what it does—move about, take in food, lie down, and so on. But do you think of your family and friends as complicated masses of cells that move and stop and then move again? I doubt it. That would be a most unusual way to think about people. Our interest is usually pitched at a different level, where deception and disappointment, hope and happiness, surprises and secrets all lie. How can the physical stuff lead such a complex life?

This complex life exists at the level of human relations. We care about what people do, how it fits with what we ourselves will do, how that affects others, and so on. We want to know why people did what they did and we wonder what they are going to do next. If this makes us

1

sound rather like psychologists, that is just what I intend.
Psychologists try to understand human behavior, to explain why people act the way they do, to predict what
people will do. In this sense, we are all psychologists.
We may not be aiming to produce general laws to explain human behavior, but we are all interested in the
way people behave. "Why did she do that?" "What will
he do next?" This is the sort of question we ask one
another every day. Of course, psychologists' explanations take a variety of forms depending on the particular
theory they hold. "She has been reinforced for producing
that behavior in the past," says one. "His brain is not
fully matured," says another. But what about the explanations we give to each other in our everyday conversations? We say, "She wanted to get such and so . . ." "He
thinks it is . . ." "She was sad because . . ." Our replies
refer to what people think and want and feel. This is our
everyday, commonsense psychology. And this is where
we must look in order to discover the mind.

This everyday psychology is often called *belief-desire
psychology* because that is what it appeals to. Here the
words "belief" and "desire" don't have their common
conversational meanings, where beliefs are things taken
on faith, such as religious convictions, and desire is lust
or longing for something. As I use the words here and
throughout the book, belief is simply taking something
as true and desire is simply wanting. For example, why
did Carl race past me this morning without stopping to
talk? Because he thought it was nine o'clock and he
wanted to get to his meeting on time; he was ashamed
he'd been late every week so far and he meant to do
better. That is, in order to explain and predict a person's
actions we refer to his beliefs, desires, emotions, and
intentions. Believing it's late, desiring to be punctual,

feeling ashamed of past performance, intending to improve—these are all states of mind. In fact, they *are* the mind. Of course, these states of mind originate in the brain, but the mind is not the brain; it is the sum of these mental states. These thoughts, wants, feelings, plans, and so on, together make up the mind—if it exists.

Why "if it exists"? Some philosophers and psychologists argue a great deal about whether such mental states really exist. As I just said, mental states originate in the brain, in neural activity. What we are calling beliefs and desires, they argue, are simply certain states of the brain. Therefore, we don't need to imagine that there is a mental level mediating between the brain and behavior. Mental states are simply brain states. Changes in behavior can be explained entirely by changes in the brain.[1]

These people may worry about whether mental states like beliefs and desires really exist. But we don't. In fact, neither do they in their everyday lives. An ardently materialist philosopher would be quite at home with my explanation of Carl's racing past me this morning—she might have said the same thing herself. Along with everybody else, these philosophers and psychologists talk about what people think, want, hope for, plan to do, and so on. Playwrights, poets, and ordinary folk have been talking like this for generations. Indeed, *folk psychology* is another name for belief-desire psychology. Folk psychology simply assumes that beliefs and desires exist. It assumes that people have minds that are the sum of their beliefs, desires, emotions, and intentions. Then it uses this assumption to explain why people act the way they do and to predict what they will do.

It has become common, recently, to call this folk psychology a *theory of mind*. The term was first used in this context by two psychologists, David Premack and Guy

Woodruff, in their research into primate intelligence.[2] One of their interests was in chimpanzees' ability to predict human action. They showed a chimpanzee videotapes in which a human actor in an animal cage faced problems trying to reach inaccessible objects, such as a bunch of bananas outside the cage. At the end of the tape they showed the animal two photographs, one giving a "solution" to the problem, such as the actor's reaching out of the cage with a stick. They found that the chimpanzee reliably chose the picture of the solution, not the other one. They interpreted these results, supported by those from other, similar experiments, as showing that chimpanzees have a theory of mind. "An individual has a theory of mind if he imputes mental states to himself and others. A system of inferences of this kind is properly viewed as a theory because such states are not directly observable, and the system can be used to make predictions about the behavior of others."[3] That is, because the chimpanzee chose one photograph rather than another, these researchers concluded that the animal attributed unseen mental states to the actor, such as wanting to get bananas, and used these to make "predictions" about his action, such as that he would reach out with a stick. From these predictions they then inferred that the animal possessed a theory of mind.

Needless to say, these rather extravagant claims generated considerable debate, in the course of which a number of philosophers suggested an experimental paradigm that would demonstrate whether someone or some animal possesses a theory of mind in Premack and Woodruff's sense.[4] Both the paradigm and the term were taken up by two developmental psychologists, Heinz Wimmer and Josef Perner, in a landmark paper that investigated children's understanding of others' minds.[5]

Since then, children's theory of mind has become a very lively area of research in developmental psychology. Researchers ask questions such as: What do children know about the mind—about deception, disappointment, surprise, happiness? Can children explain and predict people's actions by considering their thoughts and wants? Do they believe in folk psychology? These questions are the ones I will address in this book. It is a fascinating story; indeed, there are two stories.

The first is the story of how children discover the mind. In fact they have two discoveries to make. One is that people do have minds made up of thoughts, wants, and so on. I call this their discovery of *what the mind is.* The other is where those thoughts and wants come from and what effects they have. I call this their discovery of *what the mind does.* Perhaps this is putting it too simply, because the two are not really separable, yet we can think of them separately. What is the mind? It is, as I have said, beliefs, desires, emotions, intentions. Mind is the sum of these mental states, or what we can call *mental representations.* And what does the mind do? It *represents,* that is, it produces these mental states. This is beginning to sound rather technical. The important thing to remember is that the discoveries children make are not those of the cognitive psychologist but those of ordinary folk, the proverbial man or woman in the street. They may never learn the words "represent" or "representation." Nonetheless, we can describe their discoveries in this way. That is the second story.

This second story takes place in scientific psychology. It is concerned with how psychologists have gradually found out about children's understanding of the mind. The two stories—what we know about children, and how we came to know it—are obviously intertwined. In the following chapters, I will describe the development of children's theory of mind and discuss the research that underlies this description.

Piaget

I begin with Jean Piaget, because it was he who first investigated children's understanding of the mind, or at least their understanding of certain mental phenomena such as thoughts and dreams. We no longer agree with all that Piaget concluded from his investigations; nonetheless, his work is important because he was the first to ask such questions, and subsequent research has been built on this foundation. The studies were conducted early in Piaget's career and are reported in his first books, published in the 1920s.[6] Many people have told the tale of how Piaget came to make these investigations. He was not a psychologist at the beginning of his career, he was a biologist, but he was also interested in philosophical questions, particularly those concerning the nature of knowledge—what knowledge is and how it is acquired. He thought that by studying psychology, especially the acquisition of knowledge by the developing child, he could combine his interest in philosophical questions about knowledge with the scientific methods used in biology. Piaget began to study psychology in 1918, after completing a doctorate in zoology; he worked in psychological laboratories in Zurich and Paris, including a brief period of work in a psychiatric clinic. In 1921, he went to Geneva and began his long career of research into children's development. In his first studies he employed a type of interview technique he had learned in the psychiatric clinic. He questioned children about common things and common happenings and followed up wherever their responses led. He asked certain predetermined questions at the start of a conversation, but after that he allowed the child's responses to determine the course of the exchange.

The children were between about four and twelve years of age. Piaget asked them about thoughts and dreams, about what things can feel pain, what things are alive, and about the sun, the moon, and the weather. You might not think that children's understanding of astronomy and meteorology would tell us much about their understanding of the mind, but in fact it does. For one thing, in their answers to these questions children showed how they think of themselves, and what we think of the self is intimately connected with what we think of the mind. For another, it turns out that children don't make the distinction we do between people and things. They endow the moon and the wind with minds of their own—or at least they talk of what the moon knows and what the wind wants, and so on—which tells us something of their understanding of knowing and wanting, essentially mental activities.

Piaget, or one of his collaborators, asked children such questions as:

- Where do dreams come from?
- What do you think with?
- Which were first, things or names?
- How did the sun begin?
- Does the moon move?
- If you pricked this stone, would it feel it?
- Does a bicycle know when it is going?
- Why does a boat not sink?

After the initial question, the adult followed where the child's answer led. For example, Piaget asked a five-year-old, "Are dreams true?" and the child replied, "No, they are pictures we see."

"Where do they come from?"

"From God."

"Are your eyes open or shut when you dream?"

"Shut."

"Could I see your dream?"

"No, you would be too far away."

"And your mother?"

"Yes, but she lights the light."

"Is the dream in the room or inside you?"

"It isn't in me or I shouldn't see it."

"And could your mother see it?"

"No, she isn't in the bed. Only my little sister sleeps with me."[7]

Here is another example: Piaget asked a child, just turned seven, "You know what it means to think?"

"Yes."

"Then think of your house. What do you think with?"

"The mouth."

"Can you think with the mouth shut?"

"No."

"With the eyes shut?"

"Yes."

"With the ears stopped up?"

"Yes."

"Now shut your mouth and think of your house. Are you thinking?"

"Yes."

"What did you think with?"

"The mouth."[8]

Piaget was not primarily interested in what children thought about these individual phenomena, dreams, thoughts, and so on. He was concerned with a larger picture. He wanted to explain the characteristics and the overall coherence of children's thinking at different stages of development. From the children's responses to many different questions, and from observing children's talk in everyday situations and analyzing the questions they asked spontaneously, he derived a number of central concepts that could be used to characterize children's thought and its development. Three key concepts in his early books are *realism, animism,* and *egocentrism.* Taken together, these concepts can be used to describe Piaget's picture of children's understanding of the mind.

Piaget concluded that before about the age of six, young children have no appreciation of mental life at all. They are realists about psychological phenomena, he said. They do not distinguish between mental entities, such as thoughts and dreams, and real physical things. Many of the children Piaget questioned associated thinking with speaking, like the child quoted above. When Piaget asked, "What do we think with?" they replied, "With the mouth." Thought for them was like speech. Children also gave realist answers to the question "Where do dreams come from?" They thought dreams came from the night, from lamps, from the sky. They thought the dream was in the room with them, and some even thought that others would also see the dream if they were in the room. That is, childhood realism endows mental entities, such as thoughts and dreams, with physical characteristics such as a public existence and a place in the world. Children who are realists in this way cannot distinguish between things and thoughts about them. According to Piaget, "the child cannot distinguish a real house, for example, from the concept or mental image or name of the house."[9]

Conversely, Piaget said, young children think that trees and rocks, the sun and the moon, are alive. For example, he was interested in children's interpretations of parallax, such as the apparent movement of the moon as one's point of observation changes. He asked a six-year-old,

> "What does the moon do when you are out for a walk?"
>
> "It goes with us."
>
> "Why?"
>
> "Because the wind makes it go."
>
> "Does the wind know where you are going?"
>
> "Yes."
>
> "And the moon too?"
>
> "Yes."
>
> "Does it move on purpose to go out with you or because it has to go?"
>
> "It comes so as to give us light."[10]

These responses illustrate the phenomenon of childhood animism. Just as children endow psychological phenomena with characteristics of the physical world, so they make the complementary error of endowing the physical world with life, and of more importance here, with mental life. Consciousness is attributed to things that act the way they do, not in accordance with physical laws, but because of what they think and want. For example, even a nine-year-old's explanation of why a box that was hung on a doubled and twisted string turned round and round, appeals to psychology not to physics:

> "Why does it turn?"
>
> "Because the string is twisted."

"Why does the string turn too?"

"Because it wants to unwind itself."

"Why?"

"Because it wants to be unwound."

"Does the string know it is twisted?"

"Yes."

"Why?"

"Because it wants to untwist itself, it knows it's twisted!"

"Does it really know it's twisted?"

"Yes. I am not sure."

"How do you think it knows?"

"Because it feels it is all twisted."[11]

Piaget sought to explain why children conceive of the world in this way. Why does a child think that dreams come into his room from outside, that the moon follows him to see where he is going, that strings feel twisted? Piaget's answer is that children think like this because they are egocentric. He first used the term "egocentric" to describe some aspects of the child's language. In their early years, children often talk without any intention of communicating with anyone, but simply for themselves. They may repeat something they have just heard or simply talk to themselves. Even a group of small children, apparently talking together, may each be talking for him or herself alone, with no attempt to understand and respond to the others' remarks. Piaget described such talk as "egocentric" or self-centered, not in the sense that it is selfish, but in the sense that it is only for the self. The child makes "no attempt to place himself at the point of view of his hearer."[12] Indeed, children cannot do so because they have no conception of point of view. The child is not conscious of herself, of her own point of view.

When one develops awareness of the self, the subjectivity of one's own experience becomes apparent, and one can view the world objectively. Lacking this self-consciousness, children confuse the self and the world. Without subjectivity, Piaget said, children see their thoughts and dreams as part of the physical world, which leads to realism. And without objectivity, they see physical things as being like themselves, which leads to animism; physical objects are thought to have knowledge and purpose just as the child herself does.

After publishing these conclusions, Piaget turned his attention to the study of infancy, inspired partly by the early development of his own children, in order to see how the concepts of egocentrism, realism, and animism originated. Obviously, a different methodology was required. One cannot question babies; one must simply watch them. Here, Piaget's scientific training, with its emphasis on the ability to make accurate and detailed observations, was of great importance. Piaget concluded that development in infancy is crucially dependent on infants' activity, on their actions and the effects these actions produce on their surroundings. Later, Piaget again focused on older children, but he no longer relied just on verbal questioning. He used materials that the experimenter or the child could manipulate and talk about. A more important difference, from my point of view here, is the fact that Piaget was no longer so interested in children's understanding of psychological phenomena; he turned his attention to their understanding of physical phenomena. He became interested in describing the child as a folk physicist, not as a folk psychologist.

Questions of Method

The methodology of Piaget's early studies has been justifiably criticized for its reliance on verbalization, on children's ability to talk about their understanding. Not only that, the questions presuppose an ontology the adult does not really hold. Piaget asked, for example, "Where do dreams come from?" presupposing that dreams are physical objects that come from somewhere. When a young child, striving for some way to answer the question, replied, "From the sky," he was classed as a realist. Piaget's earlier, and indeed later, work has also been criticized because the questions and tasks were not placed in a context that was meaningful to the child. If our interest is in children's competence and understanding, we must be careful to ask questions that they can comprehend in situations that make sense to them. All of us fall back on folk psychological explanations when faced with phenomena we do not fully understand—only yesterday, my computer didn't want to write onto the other disk.

Beginning about twenty years ago, researchers such as Margaret Donaldson and Rochel Gelman put some of Piaget's experimental tasks into contexts that made sense to young children, even preschoolers. They showed how competent preschoolers can actually be in their thinking and reasoning about the physical world, more competent than anyone would have expected from Piaget's work. More recently, developmentalists such as John Flavell, Henry Wellman, Josef Perner, Paul Harris, and many others have investigated preschoolers' understanding of psychological concepts, again making sure that the tasks and questions are in contexts that such young children can understand. Again, we can see how competent preschoolers are, compared with the picture Piaget gave. Wellman and his colleagues have shown, for example, that very young children really do know the difference between thoughts and things. Three-year-olds can tell you the difference between a boy who is thinking about a cookie and a boy who's got a cookie. They know which boy can see, touch, share, and eat the cookie. They don't think that thoughts are real.

Questions of method are important. How are we to investigate children's understanding of the mind? What allows us to conclude that children do or do not understand this or that about the mind? First, it is important to remember that we are looking for children's common-sense understanding, the sort I talked about earlier that ordinary folk possess, and not for the sort of understanding cognitive psychologists have. Second, we are not looking for verbal descriptions of folk psychology such as philosophers might give. We don't expect children to be able to describe their theory of mind; we have to infer it. And how do we infer it? We do so using the two basic methods of developmental psychology: observation and experiment. We can watch children and listen to them as they live and talk and play in their own family surroundings, or we can design experiments and assess their understanding from what they say and do in their responses to our tasks. Of course, we do more than just observe or experiment. We have to decide what it is we want to watch or assess. And here, we are guided by our theories as to what we consider worth watching or assessing.

As I have said, Piaget's work was criticized because he relied on children's ability to verbalize their understanding in answering his sometimes peculiar questions. Subsequent experimenters have been careful to frame their problems in a meaningful context and to ask questions in terms the child understands. However, their data and conclusions are criticized by other researchers who observe children's interactions in the hurly-burly of family life. Such observations suggest that children subscribe to some version of folk psychology at a much younger age than is apparent from the experimental work. Judy

Dunn has written perceptively about this discrepancy.[13] It seems paradoxical, she says, that infants are so tuned in to people and that toddlers appear so aware of other people's behavior and emotional reactions, and yet older preschoolers fail in experimental tests of their understanding of another's point of view. It is not an issue that we can resolve easily, but it is one that needs to be kept in mind throughout the following chapters, where I will describe data from both experimental and observational sources. Sometimes information is available from only one of these sources. Where the two sources provide conflicting information I will try to mediate between them. It may be that the conflict is more apparent than real, that the experimenters and the observers are in fact simply talking about different aspects of the child's discovery of the mind.

Organization of the Book

Three themes underlie the organization of the book. The major theme is topical. It concerns the topics or content areas relating to children's theory of mind—their understanding of pretense, desire, intention, belief, and so on, their ability to talk about these things, and the effect children's understanding has on their social interactions and their readiness for formal schooling. These topics form the subject matter of the different chapters.

The second theme is chronological. Within each content area children's abilities and understanding depend on their age. The focus of the book is the period from eighteen months to five years, and each chapter considers developmental changes between these ages. When a certain topic is of particular importance at a particular age, this age is emphasized in the relevant chapter. I also include some reference to the time before eighteen months and after five years in order to show where understanding originates and to what it leads.

The third theme is theoretical. The recent expansion of research into the child's theory of mind has led to a variety of different theoretical interpretations, some of which complement and some of which compete with one another.[14] For example, there is argument whether the data are better explained by assuming a gradual development in the child's understanding between infancy and adolescence, or whether fundamental changes occur at definite points, such as eighteen months and four years. This leads to a debate over whether children actually construct a theory about the mind, or whether they understand other people on the basis of their own experiences, or whether their understanding is simply absorbed from their culture. In addressing these issues, I aim to relate the arguments to the data in a way that will illuminate the debate for newcomers and provide a useful overview for those who are already familiar with it.

In the second chapter I describe our commonsense understanding of mind in more detail, particularly our commonsense understanding of mental representation, of what the mind does. In the subsequent chapters I look at children's gradual discovery of the mind. Chapter 3 describes important precursors to the child's theory of mind that develop in infancy, particularly the ability to distinguish between people and things. Chapter 4 focuses on striking developments occurring around eighteen months of age that mark the child's initial ability to distinguish between the world and mental representations of it, to distinguish between thoughts and things. Chapter 5 discusses the relation between thoughts and words, that is, between mental states and speech acts, and looks at how we use our knowledge of mental states to predict and explain human action. The next three

chapters examine children's understanding of these relations between thoughts and actions, the links between
the mind and the world. Chapter 6 focuses on children's
understanding of desire and intention, the effects of the
mind on the world. Chapter 7 looks at their understanding of perception and knowledge, the effect of the
world on the mind. Chapter 8 focuses on their understanding of belief and deception, and their understanding of discrepancies between what is in the mind
and what is in the world. In Chapter 9 I examine the
atypical development of children with autism and question whether they develop a theory of mind. Finally, in
Chapter 10 I take up the argument of whether children
really are developing a theory about the mind. How do
they discover the mind, that is, what causes this development? And I assess what the consequences of this
discovery are—what have children acquired by the time
they are five years old and how is this fundamental to
their readiness for school?

2 / What Does the Mind Do?

Before we can look at children's discovery of the mind, at their acquisition of folk psychology, we must take a closer look at questions that were only touched on in the previous chapter: What exactly does the child have to discover and acquire? That is, what is the mind and what does it do? What is folk psychology and how do we use it to explain and predict human action?

At the outset there are two important distinctions to make. First, these questions about human action and mind have technical as well as everyday answers. They are questions that are asked by professional philosophers and psychologists, who subscribe to a variety of theories that respond to the questions in quite different ways. Those who propose one theory produce evidence and argument to support it and to refute others. In this debate, "folk psychology" is one theory among many that lay claim to truth. But this book is not concerned with that issue. All parties agree that we all use the tenets of folk psychology in our everyday lives when we speculate about our friends' actions and justify our own. Whether our folk psychological theories and our commonsense understanding of mind are *true* or not, in any scientific way, is not really relevant here. This commonsense understanding is what children acquire, regardless of its standing in the philosophical debate.

Second, folk psychology, as one position in this debate, has been very precisely described by philosophers. No one would claim that everyone who uses folk psychology could understand, let alone give, such a description. Ordinary adults hold the theory unreflectively: their explanations and predictions are guided by it, but they may not be able to expound it. And children acquire the theory unreflectively, without thinking of it as a theory. We can evaluate their understanding from the ways in which they account for and anticipate people's actions, but we cannot expect them to give a detailed account of the theory, of the rules and principles underlying their explaining and predicting. However, in order to investigate children's understanding of mind and their acquisition of folk psychology, we need a precise description of these things.

Folk Psychology

Folk psychology, as we've already seen, is concerned with explaining and predicting human behavior. The philosopher Daniel Dennett has explored the ways in which we can explain and predict what someone or something does.[1] Dennett says that if you want to explain why something does what it does and if you want to predict what it will do, there are three possible ways you could look at it. "It" may be a machine, or an animal, or a person; that doesn't matter. There are three ways you can look at it, three "stances" you might take. Let's say "it" is an alarm clock, and you want to explain why it woke you up this morning and predict what time it will wake you up tomorrow.

First, there is the *physical* stance. You could describe how the clock is made, the cogs and wheels and levers and so on. When they are set a certain way, the bell rings. However, there are lots of different kinds of alarm clocks: mechanical ones with cogs and bells, electric ones with transistors and music, electronic ones with batteries and high-pitched beeps. Each one would need a different explanation, unless we move to another stance.

The second stance we might take is the *design* stance. If we take a design stance, we can give the same explanations and make the same predictions for all the different kinds of alarm clocks. We assume the clocks have no malfunction, that is, we assume they are all working properly. Then we predict that they will behave as they are designed to behave. This is a functional level of explanation. The three kinds of clocks may need to be set in quite different ways, but if we set each of them to wake us at seven o'clock that is what they will all do.

The third stance we might take is the *intentional* stance. We treat the object or animal or person as a rational agent. We infer its beliefs and desires and predict that it will act to fulfil its desires in the light of its beliefs. This stance is obviously rather fanciful for our alarm clock example. We would have to assume that the alarm clock wanted to wake us up, it didn't want us to be late for work, and it believed that ringing its bell would do the trick. We don't need to ascribe beliefs and desires to alarm clocks in order to explain and predict what they do. But as Dennett shows, the intentional stance is sometimes the best stance to take toward a machine, such as a chess-playing computer, which is far more complicated than an alarm clock. We may understand nothing at all about its hardware, so it is impossible for us to take a physical stance toward it. We may understand nothing about its software either—how the machine is programmed, how it is designed to behave—and so we can't take a design stance toward it. However, we do understand that it was designed to beat us at chess, and so if we take an intentional stance we can predict its moves. The machine "wants" to block our check and "believes" it could do so by moving its queen, so we predict that is what it will do. This is a simple and powerful way of understanding a complicated machine. Indeed, the fact that the intentional stance works so well for understanding computers has led many people to conclude that computers think.

Although we don't usually need to take the intentional stance toward machines, it is the stance we usually take toward people. It is, of course, folk psychology. Dennett's intentional stance is the theoretical basis of folk psychology. We regard people as rational agents and we assume that they will act to fulfill their desires, given their beliefs. Perhaps it wasn't your alarm clock that woke you up at seven o'clock this morning. Perhaps it was your four-year-old child. Why did she do that? You might take a physical stance: she woke you up because she was hungry. Well, that would explain why she herself woke up, but it wouldn't explain why she climbed out of bed and came to wake you up. A physical explanation of all of that might get very complicated. It might be easier to take the intentional stance: she woke you up because she was hungry and she wanted something to eat and she believed that you would provide it.

Why is this third stance, the theoretical basis of folk psychology, called the intentional stance? It is because the beliefs and desires that the stance ascribes are *intentional* states. It was a nineteenth-century Austrian philosopher, Franz Brentano, who called such mental states intentional, reviving a term used by medieval philosophers.[2] Here "intentional" has a technical meaning, not the ordinary meaning of "deliberate" or "on purpose." (Some authors use a capital "I" to distinguish the philosophical term from the ordinary one, but this cannot be relied on because not all do so.) Brentano talked of intentionality, in this special sense, as "the mark of the mental."

This intentionality has more recently and colloquially been referred to as "aboutness." Intentional, or mental, states are always *about* something, objects and events in the world, or perhaps nonexistent things, as in "She believes the tooth fairy comes in the night," but even there the belief is about something. If you say you have a belief and I ask you what it is about, it would be odd if you were to reply, "Nothing. I just have a belief, that's all." Beliefs are beliefs about something; desires are desires for something. Intentions, in the everyday sense, are one sort of intentional state in the philosophical sense and they too are about something; intentions are intentions to do something. This calls into question whether or not emotions are intentional states. For example, drinking martinis may make you feel happy. If I ask you what you feel happy about, you could quite reasonably say, "Oh nothing. I just feel happy." Similarly one may just feel despair; it may not be about anything. Often, however, emotions are about something: I am unhappy my friend must work late tonight, but I am glad we can go out for dinner together tomorrow night. Beliefs, desires, intentions, and some emotions, then, are intentional states, and they are what are ascribed when we take the intentional stance.

An "intentional system" is anything the intentional stance works for—a person or an artifact to which we ascribe beliefs and desires in order to explain its behavior. When we take the intentional stance toward a person or an object our attitude will differ depending on whether we think the person or object in question is also taking an intentional stance to itself and to us. That is to say, we can credit systems with different levels of intentionality, as Dennett puts it. There is a *zero-order* level, but this doesn't really count, because in this case we do not give the system credit for any intentionality at all, since it has no beliefs or desires. In order to explain its behavior we have to take either a physical or a design stance toward it, as we did with the alarm clocks: It behaves the way it does because it has been made that way or because it has been conditioned that way. This is not an intentional system and the intentional stance won't explain its behavior.

The next level is first-order; a *first-order* intentional system has beliefs and desires, and we can predict its behavior by considering those beliefs and desires. However, the system has no beliefs about others' beliefs. It acts only to affect what another person does, not to affect what the other person thinks. Perhaps this could explain your four-year-old's behavior, when she woke you up at seven o'clock. She wanted something to eat, and she believed you would give it to her. She woke you up so that you would get up and make her breakfast. She didn't think about what you believed, just about what you would do. She was a first-order system.

A *second-order* intentional system not only has beliefs, it is also a recursive system; it can reflect back on itself. It has beliefs about its own beliefs and about the beliefs of others. It believes others have beliefs and desires, and it acts to affect what others think, not what others do. Or rather, it acts to affect what others do by affecting what they think. Perhaps you wanted to sleep and you told your four-year-old it was too early for breakfast. Perhaps she went away for a little while and then came back and told you the bathroom was flooded, or there was someone at the front door. You jumped out of bed and she said, "I tricked you. Can I have my breakfast?" Such a four-year-old is a second-order intentional system. Second-order systems not only have beliefs and desires, they also ascribe beliefs and desires to themselves and to others. They understand tricks, lies, secrets, and false beliefs. They adopt the intentional stance and in adopting it they can manipulate other people by manipulating their beliefs and desires.

Why does Dennett call it the intentional *stance?* Because it a place to stand, a position that one takes in ascribing beliefs and desires to the system in order to explain its actions. It leaves one uncommitted as to whether the system *really* has beliefs and desires, and whether beliefs and desires are *real.* Nonetheless, some theorists do regard beliefs and desires as real states, and they are interested in what these states really are. In the final analysis, they are brain states caused by particular patterns of activated neurons. However, even though the brain underlies the mind, we can still talk about organization at the mental level. Beliefs and desires are mental states that are represented in the mind. We are familiar enough with the notion of representation in the case of drawings or photographs. We understand that although the picture is "just" a pattern of marks on a piece of paper, it depicts something else. Similarly, beliefs and desires are "just" patterns of activation in our brain cells, but these patterns represent something else.

Mental Representation

Mental states like beliefs and desires are representations that mediate our activity in the world. They provide us with a psychological relationship to reality. In the case of physical relations there is a direct link to the way things really are, but in the case of psychological relations the link is often indirect.

What does this mean? Consider this illustration: Tom picks cherries off his tree and takes them to market. Nancy buys some and carries them home. Her children eat them. In all these cases there is some sort of physical, or material, relation between the person and the cherries: picking, taking to market, buying, carrying, eating. What about psychological relations? Tom intends to sell the cherries; Nancy thinks the cherries are ripe; the children want to eat them. In these cases there is some psychological relation between the person and the cherries: intending, thinking, wanting. What is the difference between the two cases?

There are three essential differences. First, when I talk about the cherries being picked, bought, and eaten, I can refer to them in a number of ways: the children ate cherries, the children ate fruits from Tom's trees, the children ate a type of drupe, the children ate fruits of *Prunus cerasus*. All refer to the same objects; it doesn't matter which one I use. However, when I talk about psychological relations, it does matter. Nancy believed they were cherries, she may not have believed they were fruits of *Prunus cerasus*. The children wanted cherries, not drupes. In the case of physical relations, therefore, reference is transparent: whatever way I refer to the object, the physical relation shows through, as it were—it is still the same. However, in the case of psychological relations, reference is opaque: if I refer to the object in a different way, the relation may not come through, may not hold. That is, intentional states are characterized by referential opacity.

Second, when I talk about a nonpsychological relation, the truth of what I say depends on the facts of the matter in the world. For example, "Nancy ate the cherries, which were ripe." That is true if they were and false if they were not. But when I talk of a psychological or intentional relation, such as "Nancy believed the cherries were ripe," it may be true whatever the actual state of the cherries. That is to say, in the case of physical relations, truth is accounted for, or *entailed*, by things and events in the world, but in the case of psychological relations truth is not entailed. Third, existence is entailed, or not, in a similar way. "The cherries are in the basket" is true only if there are cherries in the basket, but Nancy may believe there are cherries in the basket even if the children have eaten them all.

The proverbial man or woman in the street is unlikely to have heard of "referential opacity" and the "nonentailment of truth and existence," but will nevertheless have an intuitive understanding of these features of mental representation. Indeed, such understanding is a fundamental part of our folk psychology. It allows us to understand everyday reactions, such as someone's surprise when things turn out to be different from what was expected, and commonplace mistaken action, such as someone's looking for something in the wrong place. Such actions and reactions come about because people are indirectly related to the world through their mental representations of it, and they act on the basis of those representations even in cases where the representation does not accurately reflect reality.

Imagine this scene: A man comes home from the store with a bag of apples, which he puts into the refrigerator before he goes out to the backyard. A woman comes into the kitchen looking for something to eat. She sees the apples in the refrigerator, takes one and bites into it. Finding it too cold she moves the apples to the cupboard. Later the man returns to the kitchen. "I'm hungry," he says, "I'll have an apple." We are not surprised that he looks in the refrigerator, nor are we surprised when he finds no apples there. Our lack of surprise demonstrates some fundamental aspects of our commonsense understanding of mental representation. First, we believe there is a real world out there, a world that includes real things such as apples and refrigerators. These real things exist, and they exist independent of our thoughts about them. Second, we believe we do have thoughts about these things, and sometimes those thoughts don't reflect the way things really are in the world. However, in any case we act, not on the basis of the way things *really* are, but on the basis of the way we *think* they are. That is to say, we act in accord with our mental representation of the world.

This understanding of mental representation is fundamental to our folk psychology, to our theory of mind. It is so deeply rooted in our way of thinking that it is almost impossible for us to imagine what it would be like not to think like this. There was a time, however, when we didn't. It is not an understanding we were born with, nor is it immediately acquired. At two years of age we didn't think in this way, but by the age of five we did. What happens, then, between two and five that allows children to develop this way of thinking about the world? They come to understand mental representation. They discover the mind.

Children's Understanding of Representation

In the previous chapter I said that children have two discoveries to make about the mind: *what it is* and *what it does*. I said the mind represents—that's what it does—and the mind is the sum of these mental representations—that's what it is. Thus we can think of *representation* in two ways. "A representation" is a mental

state: thought, want, belief, intention, and so on, whereas
"representation" (without the indefinite article) is the act
of forming these mental states. Representation is thus
both an *activity* and an *entity*, both a process and a product. It is the process by which the mind produces representations.

This means that children might begin with only a
partial understanding of mental representation. They
might understand that beliefs and desires are mental
entities, separate from reality, and so would not confuse
thoughts and things. They might consider these mental
entities as unseen states that are, in a sense, possible
alternative situations to the real situation.[3] Moreover,
they could use their knowledge of these unseen states to
make predictions about people's actions. They might be
able to do all this with only a partial understanding of
representation.

A more complete understanding would include the
realization that beliefs and desires are not just things that
exist in the mind, but representations produced by the
mind that relate to the world in certain specific ways.
Some mental states are merely thoughts about things in
the world; beliefs, on the other hand, represent the world
in a particular way. Josef Perner brings this out very
clearly in his distinction between *thinking of* and *thinking
that*.[4] I can think of you working at your desk, I can think
of you lying on the beach, and I can think of you sleeping
in your bed—all possible situations—and I can think of
them all at the same time. However, I can't think *that* you
are working at your desk, *that* you are lying on the beach,
and *that* you are sleeping in your bed, all at the same
time. I can't seriously take the world to be three different
ways at once. Fundamentally, I take things to be *one way*,
and I take that way to be *true*. If I seriously think that
you are away on vacation, lying on the beach, I will be

surprised to see you in your office working at your desk. We are surprised when our beliefs turn out to be false. However, even if I know that you are away on vacation, I can still think of you in your office.

There is an important difference between this partial understanding of representation and a more complete understanding, as subsequent chapters will show. Understanding beliefs and desires as mental entities allows for all sorts of prediction and explanation of what people do. However, there are cases when it fails. An obvious case is that of mistaken action, as in the example of the man looking for apples in the refrigerator. He was not just *thinking of* apples in the refrigerator, he *thought that* the apples were in the refrigerator. If children do not understand representational activity—if they do not understand that people represent the world and take those representations to be truly the way the world is—they cannot understand such mistaken action.

When I say that children have to understand representational activity, of course I do not mean that they have to understand neuropsychological processes. Indeed, these are below conscious awareness and beyond the understanding of most adults. I simply mean that the child sees that the mind is active—it construes and interprets situations and continuously revises its interpretations in the light of changing situations—and is not just a passive holder for mental entities. This is the folk psychological distinction between the mind as a container and the mind as a processor.[5] It allows children to see that people do not have direct access to reality but construct and construe the world in their minds. Essentially, it allows children to see not only that thoughts and things are different, but also how thoughts and things are related. The man's thought was about where the apples were. That is, his belief referred to the location of the apples, which he had put into the refrigerator. Remember, however, that the woman had moved them to the cupboard, and so his thought referred to that location, to those very apples now in the cupboard. But remember also that he hadn't seen her move them to the cupboard; he thought they were still in the refrigerator. That is to say, his representation of the apples, which are actually in the cupboard, represented them as in the refrigerator.[6]

As children discover the mind, they acquire an understanding of representation in both senses, as mental entity and mental activity, in other words, as product and process. Perhaps it would be clearer if, with Perner, we did not refer to the partial understanding as *representational* at all. We could think of it as a mentalistic but non-representational understanding of belief and desire. We could. However, not everyone does, as we will see in later chapters, so we must keep these two different uses of "representation" in mind.

The Cultural Context

One further issue needs to be addressed: the extent of cultural diversity in our understanding of mental life, in our theories of mind. Is an understanding of mental representation common to all humanity? Do people everywhere believe there is a world that exists independent of their thoughts and that those thoughts may not always reflect the way things really are?

It is a trivial truism to say that different cultures are both similar and dissimilar: similar because all people have similar bodies, similar brains, and similar physiological processes, and live in a world in which the same basic laws of physics and chemistry apply; dissimilar because of the myriad differences of social organization and language. This suggests that there will be both similarities and differences in folk psychological theories in different cultures, and the data, although somewhat sparse, support this suggestion.

How could we begin to investigate the folk psychological theory of people in another culture? How could we find out about their understanding of the beliefs, desires, intentions, and emotions that are ascribed when we take the intentional stance? How could we ever know whether they attribute beliefs and desires to others to explain and predict their actions? Beliefs and desires are hidden states; they may be expressed and ascribed in language but, even if they are, variations in linguistic expression may hide underlying commonality. Perhaps for this reason crosscultural research has focused on the role of emotion in folk psychological theories. Emotions are tied to beliefs and desires but they are not hidden in the same way. They can be displayed without language in facial expression and gesture. For example, if someone's belief turns out to be false, he may show surprise, or if someone's desire is fulfilled, she may look happy, and so on. Does the production and interpretation of these nonverbal expressions occur in all cultures, and if so, does it occur in similar ways in similar circumstances?

Last century Charles Darwin claimed that the facial expression of emotion and the recognition and understanding of such expressions are innate, universal characteristics of humankind.[7] Psychologists have since attempted to assess Darwin's claim by investigating the production and recognition of different facial expressions by people of very different cultures and by young infants. For example, Paul Ekman and his colleagues have shown that people from a variety of cultures, both literate and nonliterate, can produce and recognize expressions of six basic emotions, what we would call happiness, anger, sadness, disgust, fear, and surprise, although these last two were sometimes confused.[8] In these studies, people listened to a story in which a character would be likely to experience one of these emotions, such as happiness, and then they either chose a photograph of a happy face from a number of photographs showing different expressions or they mimicked a happy face when they were asked to show how the story character would feel. Other researchers have shown that quite early in life babies produce expressions of these different emotions and appear to recognize at least some of them from a fairly young age (see Chapter 3).[9] Thus, it seems Darwin was right in suggesting an innate and universal basis for at least some emotions.

However, anthropologists have also described differences in the emotions recognized by people from different cultures. If we were to compare English terms for emotions with those in other languages, we would find that some peoples use a single word for emotions that are distinguished in English, some distinguish several emotions where there is only one term in English, and some have a single word for an emotion that can only be paraphrased in English. Furthermore, anthropologists suggest that some cultures have emotion concepts that appear to have no equivalent in English. For example, the Ifaluk of Micronesia experience *fago,* a sort of blend of compassion, love, and sadness.[10] Nevertheless, in all these cases one can have some understanding of the words and concepts of another culture in terms of the basic emotions that appear to be shared among all cultures. It seems that children everywhere experience these basic emotions and are able to recognize them and attribute them to others. More complex emotions, particular to a culture, are acquired and understood during development, as children acquire the emotion theory of their culture.[11]

What then of the folk psychologies that these emotion theories are part of? Is belief-desire psychology universal or is it unique to Western culture? Again, it appears there is a basic sameness underlying cultural differences, reflecting the basic similarity of our physical selves that underlies the very different features of our social systems.[12] People everywhere try to explain their own actions and to understand the actions of others in terms of the moral code of their society. This suggests that there is general recognition of the self, and of the self as distinct from others and from the physical world. That is to say, self-awareness is a universal human characteristic. What is variable is how control of the self's actions is conceptualized, where the locus of control is perceived to be. Does it lie within the person or with some external force?

In Western culture we consider that it is internal: people control their own action and are responsible for its outcome. Our practice of assigning praise and blame, our legal justice system, and our understanding of the emotions of pride, shame, and guilt all depend on this. Such an understanding of the internal cause of action is acquired at an early age. As parents will testify, asking "Why?" is a favorite occupation of preschoolers, who can understand and explain why someone did something in terms of internal states, such as what the person wanted or intended. They can also justify their own actions by appealing to their intentions. Judy Dunn quotes a boy, not quite three years old, who responded to his mother's command to get off the sofa by telling her that he was trying to clean the television: "I going try and get a paint off. All I'm trying to do is—there."[13] Later, in school, Western children may acquire a more technical understanding of internal control as they learn about the brain and mind. But even before that they may be told to "use your brain" or hear rhymes such as this on "Sesame Street":

I have a mind and my mind helps me,
In everything I do and see.

Technical concepts, only partly understood, appear in adults' reasoning too—for example, in appeals to the Freudian idea of unconscious impulses to explain actions. Such sources are internal, although beyond personal control. Middle-class American adults, asked why they went into their profession, may explain their choice by referring to tenets of popular Freudian psychology.[14] But sometimes, as when we appeal to astrology, we may assign control outside the person: "It was in the stars." Even those of us who firmly believe in an internal locus of control may consult our horoscope in the newspaper each morning. In non-Western cultures, the idea of external agents of control may be more prevalent. The Dinka of southern Sudan, for example, do not share our notion of self-responsibility and have no conception of our emotion of guilt. They have a concept that corresponds to conscience (*mathiang gok*), but it is an external force. It acts from outside the person and may be employed by someone else; for example, if someone has not paid a debt, the creditor may inflict *mathiang gok* on the debtor.[15]

At the present time there is little cross-cultural research in the development of folk psychologies, but I will refer to what studies there are in subsequent chapters. Various cultures seem to recognize similar stages of childhood. For example, Fijians acknowledge the end of infancy when their children acquire *vakayalo* (sense) at two years of age, and the Inuit Utku when their children acquire *ihuma* (reason) at two; Americans mark two-year-olds' new independence by recognizing the beginning of the "terrible twos."[16] Similarly, in many cultures children are considered to be ready for formal education when they are five or six years old. Many of the developments discussed in subsequent chapters, as children, in Western terms, discover the mind, are fundamental to this readiness for schooling.

3 / People and Things

When do children first begin to discover the mind? Do toddlers, even babies, know anything about the mind? We look at a newborn baby, her head flops to one side, her eyes don't focus on ours. Can she think? What is she thinking? How much does she understand? We wonder about these things but we talk to her as though she does understand. And one wonderful day two or three months later her eyes meet ours and a smile lights her face. Now it is easy to treat her as a real person. But what does she think and want and feel? How much does she know about herself and about us, about her thoughts and feelings and about ours? What is it like to be a baby?

The First Months

These are very old questions. The last twenty-five years, however, have produced many new answers. Developmental psychologists have found new ways to ask these questions so that very young babies, even newborns, can answer them.[1] They still can't tell us directly, of course, but from the very beginning infants can suck, can look, and can turn their heads to either side when they are lying down. These three responses have been used by researchers to find out what babies know and want. For

36

instance, what do they like to look at? Do they prefer some things over others? If we put different things on either side of a baby's head while he is lying down, will he look at one more than the other? If the two things smell different can he discriminate between them? If a baby doesn't appear to prefer one thing over the other, can she tell them apart? We can ask this using a *habituation/dishabituation* paradigm. We keep showing her the same thing time and time again until she is bored with it and doesn't look at it for very long; she is habituated to it. Then we show her something different. Does she spend longer looking at the new thing or does she seem as bored with it as the one she has seen repeatedly? If she spends longer, that is, if she dishabituates, we know it seems different to her from what she was looking at before.

Our questions then become: What do babies like to look at and to listen to? What sorts of changes do they notice in their surroundings? And most important, what does this tell us about their understanding of people and their discovery of the mind?

From the very beginning, babies notice and appreciate people, or, in the language of the laboratory, they prefer social to nonsocial stimuli.[2] We can tell this from psychological experiments and we also know it from our own experience. As soon as the baby is able to turn her head, we can see that she follows us as we move about the room and we recognize the pleasure she seems to derive from face-to-face contact. But what does she see? Does she know who it is she sees?

A lot of research effort has recently been put into investigations of infants' perception of the human face. The features of faces—light and dark contrast, movement, three-dimensionality—are exactly the features that infants prefer in visual discrimination experiments.

Much of this work has used schematized drawings of the face, which gives experimenters precise control over the stimuli. Although some researchers have found that two-month-olds prefer a face over other patterns of equal complexity, generally this work has shown that babies don't reliably show this preference until four or five months of age. However, research using real faces, which are moving and three-dimensional as well as having contrast and complexity, has shown that much younger infants, even those two or three days old, can discriminate between their mother's face and that of a stranger.

Newborns can also distinguish their mother's voice from that of someone else. Babies can hear everything we hear. They are startled by sudden noises and soothed by rhythmic music, but it is human voices they really seem to listen to. A crying baby may stop crying when he hears his mother's voice; another baby, lying quietly, may start to kick excitedly when her father starts to talk to her. Looking at faces, listening to voices, babies seem "tuned in" to people right from the start. They are born that way.

This is not to suggest that newborns can actually tell the difference between one person and another, and between people and things, in the sense that they *know* it is their mother, that they have a concept of the person. Rather, the characteristics of people are the very ones that attract their attention, and they can detect differences among these characteristics. It is not that all their understanding is innate but that they have innate predispositions, and these help them to distinguish one person from another and from other things in the world. People and things differ in a variety of ways, although they share features too: people have faces but so do dolls; people move but so do leaves in the breeze; people talk but, in a sense, so do radios; people respond contingently, that is, depending on what the baby does, but so may a pet dog or cat. A person is characterized by a certain cluster of features. During the first months of life babies gradually come to understand that only a person has a face, moves, talks and responds to them. This development is important to the child's discovery of the mind, because people have minds, objects don't. Many of the milestones in the first year are associated with making this distinction between people and things, with acquiring a concept of the person that will eventually lead to discovering the mind.

An important milestone is the first smile, the first real smile, at about two-and-a-half to three months of age. Babies younger than this will smile in their sleep. When they are awake and alone, they will smile at things they see or hear. But real social smiles are only produced in response to another person's smile and these, of course, engender further smiles. This is the first true social interaction. About half a year later another important milestone is reached. In the beginning the baby will smile at anyone who smiles at her, but gradually she saves her best smiles for the person who takes daily care of her, often her mother. And by seven or eight months of age she may not smile at strangers, and she may be anxious and cry when her mother leaves her sight. Now she not only knows people, but she knows individual persons, and she is attached to one person more than to others. This attachment provides a secure base for the child's exploration of the world and marks a new emotional responsiveness.

The End of the First Year

Experimental research has shown that five-month-olds are able to distinguish different expressions of emotion, such as a smile and a frown.[3] However, this may not be a sign of emotional responsiveness. It may be simply a response to different visual appearances; the expressions may have no meaning for the child. A few months later, the baby can respond to their meaning.[4] This is seen, for example, in experiments using the "visual cliff," an apparatus devised to investigate infants' perception of depth. The transparent glass cover is quite level but the patterned surface underneath drops suddenly some depth below the glass. At the age when they can crawl, babies perceive this drop and are reluctant to continue crawling on the level glass surface above it. In such a situation their behavior can be influenced by the expression on their mother's face. If she smiles cheerfully the baby is encouraged to crawl over the glass but if she looks fearful he will not cross. The baby is guided by his mother's expression only in times of uncertainty. If the patterned surface is flat under the glass, that is, if there is no apparent drop, babies don't check the mother's face or, if they do, will cross whatever expression she has. That is, babies use this *social referencing* as the phenomenon has been called, to decide how to act in times of uncertainty. A baby will also check his mother's face if he encounters an unknown person or a strange new toy. If she looks hostile or fearful he will retreat, but if she appears friendly or happy he will be encouraged to approach the person or toy. Thus, children show an awareness of their mothers' emotional reactions, or at least they show an ability to respond in different ways to things in the world depending on their mother's facial expressions of emotion.

Before nine months of age babies play with toys and other objects and interact with people, smiling and babbling. But after this age a new stage is reached. Social referencing marks their ability to coordinate their interaction with a person and with objects; they are able to respond to their mother's reaction to an object in the world. A three-month-old will smile and coo at another person and a six-month-old will reach out and pick up a toy. But by nine months of age babies are no longer limited to interacting just with a person or just with things; they are able to coordinate the two, an ability that is essential for communicating with others about things in the world.

This ability is seen in social referencing but it is seen in other ways too. If the mother looks at something, the baby will follow the direction of her gaze so that both mother and baby are looking at the same thing.[5] Later, the baby can look where her mother points and can herself point to things she wants her mother to see.[6] These are all ways in which mother and baby can share one another's focus on an object, a prerequisite for communicating about it. Typically once we have focused on a topic in a conversation, we take turns talking about it. Babies also acquire these turn-taking abilities before they are actually able to converse in the conventional sense. This is seen very early on when two-month-olds engage in face-to-face interaction with their mothers: infant and mother take turns smiling and cooing at one another. There is some debate, however, over how much control of the interaction the baby has at such an early age. Some researchers, such as Rudolph Schaffer, argue that the mother fits her turns into pauses in the baby's activity.[7] Others, such as Colwyn Trevarthen, claim that even two-month-old infants are truly taking turns with the mother and are innately predisposed to such intersubjectivity.[8] Nevertheless, it is generally agreed that babies' interactions with others change in nature around nine months of age. We can see this change in the games of give and take that babies love to play at this age. Father holds out a ball, baby takes it, then gives it back to him, and back and forth it goes. She shares his focus and participates in the exchange, just as in years to come they will share a topic of conversation and talk back and forth about it.

There really is a different "feel" to one's interactions with an infant at this stage. There is a genuine sense of communication and of intention on the infant's part. But perhaps the more important issue from my point of view here is how aware such young children are of what they are doing and sharing. Are they aware of their beliefs and desires and those of others? No one would deny that infants have beliefs and desires. We can see their surprise when something unexpected happens—when a belief is not confirmed—and we witness their rage when a desire is frustrated. And when infants communicate these states to others, their behavior appears to be intentional. If a baby wants something and her mother does not immediately respond, she will persist in her attempt to get it. She will look back at her mother and look at the toy again, she will add a wanting sound to her reaching gesture, she will make the sound louder, and so on and on, until her goal has been obtained. These are all the marks of intentional activity. However, merely *possessing* beliefs, desires, and intentions is different from an *understanding* of belief, desire, and intention and the ability to attribute such states to others. Nonetheless, infants do respond to others' expressions of belief and desire. Mother says, "Look at the truck," as she points and looks, and baby looks too. Father says, "Give me the ball," holding out an open hand, and baby hands it over. Babies of this age, around the end of their first year, really are active participants in the social exchange, even though we still have real and important questions about how much understanding they have of this social interaction.

Intentional Communication

Social interaction is really an interaction of minds, of mental states, but we have to communicate those states to others. We have to let the other person know we want something, or that we want them to believe something, and so on. Human beings are not mind readers, not in any telepathic sense anyway, and in order to know what is in another person's mind we have to give that information to one another. We have to "get in touch" or "put it over" or "get it across"—these are all common ways of referring to the communication that is basic to social interaction—and this communication frequently, although not exclusively, involves language. The cover design of George Miller and Philip Johnson-Laird's book *Language and Perception* neatly conveys the idea: two profiles face one another with an arch formed of a jumble of letters of the alphabet between them.[9] In one head all the letters are green, in the other they are all red, and in the arch that spans the space between them there is a mix of green and red letters. You have your thoughts, your beliefs, desires, and so on, and I have mine. We share them in language, in the talk that passes between us.

I do not want to digress too far into a topic that has been thoroughly researched and reported in recent years, that of children's acquisition of language.[10] Nonetheless, insofar as we share our beliefs and desires in language, children's acquisition of language is fundamental to their discovery of the mind. What is important is not so much the acquisition of the meaning of particular words or the ability to string words together in acceptable ways; rather, it is the ability to use language to "get in touch" with one another and "get it across" to another. In the terms of child language textbooks, the relevant issue here is not one of acquiring semantics or syntax, but *pragmatics*, that is, learning to use language.

The study of language acquisition inspired by the Chomskyan revolution in the 1960s focused first on questions of syntax and then on semantics.[11] At the end of the decade a new breed of child language researcher emphasized the importance of pragmatic, or functional, considerations in studies of language acquisition.[12] From their point of view it didn't seem sufficient to consider just the syntactic form and semantic content of children's speech. Because language is acquired in a social context, they thought consideration should also be given to its use as a communication system, to the intentions of language users, and to the way those intentions are coded and interpreted. Indeed, not only did they give consideration to such factors, they showed that such development came before semantic and syntactic development. That is, babies communicate before they talk, an unsurprising statement to any parent.

Before they can talk, babies use other gestures as well as the previously mentioned pointing. Often these gestures develop from actions that are not at first communicative, or at least, not intended to be so.[13] For example, a baby reaches for a toy in an attempt to grasp it, someone seeing her trying to reach it passes it to her, and gradually the reach and openhanded grasping movement develop into a gesture for requesting an object. Similarly, the arm-raising gesture by which babies ask to be picked up gradually develops.[14] At first when the mother lifts the baby, his arms go up simply because her hands are in his armpits. This is just a movement, unintended and uncaused by the child. At a later stage he may cooperate in being picked up; as his mother lifts him he actively raises his arms. Still later, when his mother has no thought of picking him up, he may raise his arms to her asking to be picked up.

Thus when children begin to use language they are already effective communicators. Starting to talk is a gradual process that develops smoothly from these earlier abilities and builds on them. As babies gesture they babble and then use idiosyncratic strings of sounds that later become recognizable words, at first single words, very much tied to the situation, and later multi-word combinations. For example, the baby's reaching gesture may first be combined with babbling, then with a sound that is his expression of wanting something. Later he will use a word for the thing he wants,[15] and at this stage he can indicate precisely what he means even if the object is out of sight.

One of the most obvious and the most mysterious things about our use of language is that we *mean* something by it. How can a string of sounds mean anything, and how could a child ever acquire the notion that it does? The philosopher Paul Grice has shed light on this mystery in the distinction he makes between *natural* and *non-natural* meaning.[16] Some things "naturally" have meaning in the sense that smoke means fire, or a very young baby's crying means he is in distress. The smoke and the crying mean something and communicate something to us, although no one intends to communicate anything. The young baby simply cries and his distress is communicated to his parents, but at this early stage it implies no intention on the baby's part. Non-natural meaning, on the other hand, is the basis of intentional communication. The message—sounds, words, marks, or whatever—is intended to communicate something. In fact, there is a complex intention involved. To paraphrase Grice, intentional communication consists of one person intending to cause another person to think something or do something, simply by intending the other person to recognize from the message itself that he intends them to think or do that thing. I may cry because I am distressed, and if you hear me you may know I am distressed, although I may not even know you are there. Just like the young baby's cry, this is not an intentional communication. On the other hand, I may know that you are listening and I may want you to think I am distressed, so I cry, intending you to recognize that I want you to know I am distressed. This is a case of intentional communication, of non-natural meaning.

In his book *Child's Talk* Jerome Bruner clearly conveys how children acquire the ability to communicate intentionally in this sense, how they come to understand and to produce non-natural meanings.[17] His thesis is that they build on the natural meanings they at first produce. Their early crying naturally means they are upset, and their early reaching naturally means they want the object they are trying to get. Even though the child has no intention of communicating distress or desire at this early stage, the parent acts as though she did. That is, parents treat unintentional, natural meanings as intentional communications. Within the context of this supportive situation the child gradually acquires the ability to communicate intentionally, to convey non-natural meanings. She acquires the conventions of the system.

Isn't it sufficient simply to say that? Because language is a conventional system, wouldn't it be easier just to say that the baby learns the conventions of the system? For example, I want you to give me the ball. According to Grice's formulation, in saying "give me the ball" I intend to make you give it to me simply by getting you to see that is what I intend. Wouldn't it be easier just to say that linguistic meaning is conventional and that by convention "give me the ball" means I want you to give me the ball? True. But not enough. For I might say, "Can you give me the ball?" and I don't want you to respond "Yes." Or I might say, "Why don't you give me the ball?" and I don't want you to give me a reason. I might even say, "I can't reach the ball." These indirect requests also convey the message "give me the ball." Much of the time our communication does not rest on what our words conventionally and literally mean. Grice's theory of non-natural meaning, based on the mutual awareness of complex intentions, allows us to account for all the times when the words that are spoken do not correspond exactly and conventionally to what the speaker means. It was designed to explain the ways in which we may say one thing and mean something else. It allows us to account for all the nonliteral uses of language—for indirect requests, sarcasm, irony, and so on.

However, if we accept Grice's complicated formulation, it implies that when father says "give me the ball" and baby hands it over, she is aware of his intention that she give him the ball. That is, she is not just expressing her own intentions, by reaching out, for example, but she is aware of others' intentions. This suggests that infants know a lot about the mind. Many researchers doubt, however, that their understanding is so explicit at this early stage. Even those who first pointed out these implications from infants' communicative abilities, did not claim that infants were *aware* of the theory they were implicitly using, or that they could actually *ascribe* mental states to others.[18] Infants have an implicit theory of mind, they said, in the same way that two-year-olds have an implicit theory of grammar. Moreover, it is not until much later that children understand metaphor, irony, and so on, which depend on an understanding of Gricean principles.[19] Perhaps it is a fruitless argument.

Whether children's discovery of the mind takes them from a point of no understanding to one of understanding, or from a more implicit to a more explicit understanding, it is an important developmental process and one that is fascinating to trace.

Undoubtedly, even the one-year-old participates in the system, and not merely by rote. Young children may not understand irony, but even they don't confuse genuine "Why?" questions with indirect requests such as "Why don't you put your toys away?" They never answer the latter with "Because . . .," at least not until later and cheekier years. As Bruner has suggested, this indicates that children recognize the different intentions behind the two forms. They are learning about *communication*, not about *interrogatives*. Their focus is on the intentional aspect of language, on what people mean. Indeed, as Margaret Donaldson has pointed out, in a sense they understand what people mean before they understand what the words mean.[20] She tells the story of an English woman sitting with an Arab woman and her two children, a seven-year-old boy and a thirteen-month-old girl. The English woman speaks only English, and mother and son only Arabic. The little girl can speak neither. She toddles to the English woman and back to her mother, then she turns to walk to the English woman again, who points to the boy and says, "Walk to your brother this time." He opens his arms and the baby goes to him. The boy didn't comprehend the woman's words, but he understood the situation and so did his sister. Donaldson's point is that what was meant was so clear from the situation that the children appeared to understand the words. This is how children learn to use language. However, at this early stage their understanding is embedded in the context, in the here and now. After infancy they start to go beyond the immediate present, beyond the here and now, and this is the topic of the next chapter.

4 / Thoughts and Things

The focus on infancy research in the last twenty-five years and the many investigations of infants' social and communicative skills, show us that babies know a lot more and understand a lot more than psychologists used to think they did. However, no one would deny that babies and young preschoolers are very different creatures, different in many ways, and different in their understanding of the mind. What is the basis of that difference? To put it very simply, babies are well able to think about things in the world, to think about reality, but they don't think of alternative possible or hypothetical realities. A dramatic change occurs around the middle of the second year when they begin to think about alternatives to reality. Then they are not limited to thinking about the world only as it is presented to them. They can also think about absent and hypothetical situations.

The End of Infancy

How do we know this? The experimental work from which this knowledge is derived began with Piaget's observations of his own three children and continued in subsequent investigations built on his work.[1] What sorts of tasks have investigators used? We put a bright doll just out of one-year-old Joe's reach and leave a toy rake nearby. Joe waves his arms around, wanting the doll. His hand hits the rake and he picks it up. He waves the rake around and it hits the doll. He waves it some more, and it pulls the doll nearer to him. Then he reaches out and grabs the doll. Now let's try it with Molly, who is nearly two years old. We put the doll out of her reach, leaving the rake nearby. She looks at the doll, she looks at the rake, she looks back at the doll. Then she picks up the rake and scoops the doll toward herself. Joe and Molly have both achieved the same end, although Joe's motto seems to be "If at first you don't succeed, try, try, again," and Molly's "Look before you leap." Tasks like these show us that sometime in the middle of their second year children acquire the ability to think out a solution to a new problem, to solve it with "insight," without going through a period of trial and error. The child is able to imagine possible ways of acting and then to act.

Let's try something else. Here is a bunch of brightly colored plastic keys. I rattle them and show them to Joe, who is interested in them. I close my hand round them, hiding the keys, and as he watches I put my hand under a pillow on the sofa. Leaving the keys behind, I bring my hand out, still closed, and say to Joe, "Where are the keys?" He opens my fist—no keys. Now he doesn't know where to look; he can't find them. But Molly can, even when I "invisibly displace" them by hiding them in this complicated way. Joe can remember that the keys were in my hand, but he is lost when it turns out to be empty, whereas Molly can think back and remember my hand under the pillow and can work out that the keys might be there. She can imagine their probable location.

Joe knows one or two words, but Molly talks more than he does, and she's not bound to the here and now in the way that Joe is. She can talk about objects that aren't right there; she can ask for something she can't see, and she will go and fetch something from another room if we ask her for it. In simple ways she can talk about things that happened in the past. Emily, a little girl who was audiotaped as she talked to herself in her crib, gives us many examples—at twenty-one months, for instance, she reflected on an incident that had happened earlier in the day:

> Car broke,
> the . . . Emmy can't go in the car.
> Go in green car . . .[2]

Children of this age can also think ahead to something they plan to do, act on the plan, and then comment on its success or failure—*there* to mark success, and *oh dear* or *uh-oh* to mark failure—quite unsophisticated comments perhaps, but comments nonetheless.[3] For example, a child might plan to build a tower, smile and say "there" as she completes it, or if it falls as she adds the last block she might say "uh-oh." Her *uh-oh* indicates the discrepancy between what she imagined and what actually happened: she can think of the possibility and compare it with the reality.

Thus, in all these ways—talking about events gone by and things out of sight, solving problems by insight, finding invisibly displaced objects—children in their second year of life show us that they can think about absent and hypothetical situations. All of these behaviors, which develop around eighteen months of age, show that the child can think about possible states of affairs, not just about things that actually exist before her eyes, in front of her. This ability—to imagine a possible alternative reality—is perhaps most clearly seen in young children's pretend play, which also begins to develop at about this age.

Pretend Play

It was Piaget who first made much of young children's ability to pretend.[4] He described his daughter Jacqueline, at fifteen months of age, pretending to go to sleep, holding a cloth in the way she usually held her pillow, sucking her thumb and lying down, but laughing and saying "no, no," knowing this wasn't real sleep. Another daughter, at nineteen months of age, "pretended to drink out of a box and then held it to the mouths of all who were present."[5] No parent, indeed no one who has spent time with young children, will need an elaboration of these descriptions. They are familiar to us all. Children everywhere play in this way, although the amount of make-believe play varies in different cultural and social groups, and among individual children.[6]

Children's make-believe play is delightful to observe. Here we really see the child's ability to imagine possible, hypothetical worlds—an ability that begins around eighteen months of age and develops remarkably over the next few years. However, even children just two years old can get involved in quite complicated pretend scenarios, as this example shows:

> J. finds an enclosure made from blocks. He picks up a small figure with a wide-brimmed hat on: "Farmer want a bath. Gonna give farmer a bath." J. pretends to turn on imaginary faucets at one end of the enclosure. He swishes the figure around briefly, then says, "Oh, no, soooooo hot. Gotta put some cold in." He makes the farmer figure get out and pretends to add some more water from the imaginary faucets. J. then puts the farmer back into the "bath."

"Oh, no, soooooo hot, too hot. Ouch. Gotta put some cold in." He makes the figure hop out of the bath again.[7]

By three or four years of age, children's pretend play becomes quite complex and inventive and may occupy much of their playtime.[8] Children take on make-believe roles and act out complicated scenarios in make-believe places. Even two-year-olds can play like this if they are supported by an older and friendly sibling, as Judy Dunn's observations have shown.

John's sister:	I know, you can be the daddy and I can be the mummy. Yes?
John:	Yes.
John's sister:	Right, we've got a baby haven't we?
John:	Yeah.
John's sister:	(addresses him by real father's name) Henry.
John:	Yeah?
John's sister:	Have you got any babies?
John:	(inaudible reply)
John to observer:	I a daddy.[9]

John, who is just two years old, could not only take on a pretend identity and play appropriately in that role, he was also able to tell someone else that was who he was pretending to be. And two-year-old children explicitly label pretending with the word "pretend": "He pretending himself is a beetle," "Those monsters are just pretend, right?" "I going out Mommy. Mommy you (pre)tend to cry."[10]

Moreover, it is not just in pretend play that children can imagine things and talk about pretense. Three-year-old Katie was walking home from daycare with her mother:

> *Mother:* What shall we have for dinner?
>
> *Katie:* Daddy.
>
> *Mother:* That's a good idea, yes, with ketchup.
>
> *Katie:* Let's have Mommy for dinner.
>
> *Mother:* With ketchup?
>
> *Katie:* Yes.
>
> *Mother:* But then Mommy would be eaten all up. I'd be all gone if you had me for dinner.
>
> *Katie:* (looking upset) It's just pretend.

These observations of children's play and talk in everyday situations are supported by the recent experimental work of Paul Harris and Robert Kavanaugh.[11] In these studies the authors could control the situation and demonstrate that two-year-olds really do understand another person's pretense, they are not just carried along in the game. For example, if her child is playing with a toy tea set, a mother may hold out a cup asking for some "tea," and the child may pick up the teapot and pretend to pour into the cup. However, in the context this may be the most obvious thing to do, or the child may simply be imitating what her mother or sister just did. Harris and Kavanaugh designed their experiments so that children's appropriate responses gave evidence of real understanding. If the experimenter pretended that a yellow block was a banana and a red block was cake, and then told two-year-olds that the pig wants some cake, or the duck wants some banana, the children appropriately gave the toy animals a red block or a yellow one from a pile of blocks. And they could use the same "prop," for example a popsicle stick, to stir the teddy bear's tea or brush the teddy bear's teeth, depending on the experimenter's request. They could also act appropriately and describe the action within a pretend scenario. If the experimenter made a naughty puppet pour make-believe tea over one of the toy pigs, the child would dry the pig that was all wet and could explain what had happened. None of this is remarkable. We have all seen two-year-olds doing these things. However, Harris and Kavanaugh show that two-year-olds' competence and understanding is as good in a controlled situation as we have assumed it is from watching their everyday play.

What Can We Learn from Children's Pretend Play?

The important question is: What does children's ability to pretend tell us about their understanding of the mind? Again, it was Piaget who first attempted to answer this question. According to him, pretense shows the development of the child's capacity for symbolic representation, that is, the ability to use one thing to stand for another. For example, when Jacqueline pretended that a cloth was her pillow, she was using the cloth as a symbol for the pillow, and in saying "no, no" she indicated that she was aware of what she was doing—she understood that the cloth represented the pillow. The objects the young child first uses in pretend play, Piaget said, are personal symbols. That is, at the beginning children's pretense is solitary; later it becomes social and symbols become shared.

In contrast, Alan Leslie has emphasized that from the beginning, when children first start to pretend, they are able to understand pretense in others, as Dunn's observations and Harris and Kavanaugh's experiments have shown. Therefore the importance of early pretense, Leslie says, is that it is the first clear sign of children's ability to understand another person's mental state.[12] This must be so if they can coordinate their pretending with that of another person, because they have to link their actions to what the other person is pretending, not what he or she is actually doing. Leslie's concern is to explain how such young children acquire this understanding. He wonders why two-year-olds aren't confused by pretense. They are at an age when they are just finding out about the world and about the meaning of words, and one would think that pretense would distort all of that. Consider, he says, a two-year-old watching her mother using a telephone; she doesn't understand what it is for or how it works, but she is acquiring knowledge that will build up that understanding. Then her mother pretends that a banana is a telephone. Leslie wonders what would happen if the child treated this information in the same serious way as before—it could lead to some strange ideas. Then the mother hands the child the banana, saying "Here, take the telephone." Now language learning is in danger too![13] So why don't two-year-olds get hopelessly confused by pretense? Leslie proposes that the brain has a special innate mechanism, what he calls a Theory of Mind module, that enables the child to isolate pretense from the real world.[14]

Our perceptual and cognitive systems have evolved to allow us to form correct representations, that is, true beliefs, about the world—easy enough to say although incredibly hard to describe and explain, but *how* this is achieved doesn't matter here. Suffice it to say we all assume it is what happens—seeing is believing, after all. Leslie calls these correct representations of the world *primary representations*. The cognitive system forms these primary representations from infancy onward—even a baby can see the curved yellow banana, for example, as the evidence in the previous chapter showed. However, we don't just have primary representations, beliefs about the world, we also have beliefs about our own and others' beliefs (and hopes, fears, desires, intentions, and pretenses). That is, we have beliefs about beliefs, what Leslie calls *secondary representations*. These beliefs are different from primary representations in important ways, because, as we saw in Chapter 2, such beliefs are opaque, that is, they are suspended from reality, and don't carry the same truth and existence implications that primary representations do. "The cherries are ripe" implies both that there are cherries and that they are ripe. However, "*Nancy thinks* the cherries are ripe" may be true whether the cherries are actually ripe or not, or even if they have all been eaten. Here, we take Nancy's primary representation, "The cherries are ripe," and embed it in the secondary representation, "Nancy thinks the cherries are ripe." Embedding it in this way suspends its truth and existence implications. According to Leslie, the Theory of Mind module is the cognitive mechanism that performs this embedding. Once the primary representation is embedded in this way it is isolated from reality, neither true nor false.

Leslie argues that children's pretend play is the first sign of this system in action. It allows the child to form secondary representations of the sort "*John pretends* he is a daddy" or "*I pretend* the banana is a telephone," without the child's cognitive system confusing the properties of little boys and fathers, or bananas and telephones. The "knowing looks and smiles" that Piaget remarked on,[15] like the exaggerated actions and special tone of voice we use, provide social clues that we are pretending, but, according to Leslie, the cognitive mechanism underlying this is innate. Later, the mechanism can form other secondary representations, using *think*, for example, "I think that is a porkypine," "You think it don't belongs to me."[16] Leslie calls these secondary representations *metarepresentations*. He uses the prefix *meta-* to indicate their recursive nature—they are secondary representations of primary representations.

Josef Perner agrees with Leslie that two-year-olds' ability to pretend shows that they can form secondary representations, suspended from reality, but he does not agree that they should be called metarepresentations.[17] Perner argues against Piaget's interpretation of pretend play as showing the onset of the capacity for symbolic representation. He denies that such young children understand representation. For Perner, young children's pretense shows that they can imagine alternative hypothetical situations and act "as if" the world were that way. Being able to understand that something could be something else, that a cloth, for example, could be a pillow, does not require understanding that something can be used to *represent* something else, Perner says.

This is a very important point, because two-year-olds cannot understand misrepresentation even though they understand pretense. They cannot understand the sort of things discussed in Chapter 2, for example, why a person would look for something in the place where he thought it was, not in the new place it had been moved to while he wasn't looking. If young children have a representational understanding of pretense, we would expect that they would understand misrepresentation, which also requires representational understanding. Yet children do not understand misrepresentation until age four, and Perner says we should not credit them with metarepresentational understanding until then.

It is confusing that researchers use the term metarepresentation in different ways. It reflects the different senses of representation I discussed in Chapter 2, where I said that children have to discover two things about the mind: what it is and what it does. The mind represents—that's what it does. And it is the sum of these mental representations—that's what it is. Thus, representation has two senses: a representation is a mental entity, such as a belief, and representation is the mind's activity in forming beliefs and other mental states. The two different senses of "metarepresentation" reflect these two different ways of thinking about representation. Metarepresentations, in Leslie's sense, are representations of representational entities, such as beliefs about beliefs. Metarepresentation, in Perner's sense, is an understanding of representational activity—not of course in any neurophysiological way—that allows the child to see mental states *as* representations.

It may be, however, that children's ability to pretend implies less than either Leslie or Perner claim. Harris and Kavanaugh offer another way of thinking about it. They agree with Leslie that children must link their actions to what the other person is pretending, not what he or she is actually doing. But they do not agree that this shows that the child understands the other person's mental state. They suggest, as Angeline Lillard[18] has done, that the child recognizes a "distinctive form of action rather than a distinctive mental stance of pretending."[19] Two-year-olds may think of pretense as a special kind of activity, rather than thinking about the mental states involved—as representations or as hypothetical situations or as anything else. Harris and Kavanaugh propose a model in which understanding pretense is analogous to comprehending a story. In both cases comprehension is a constructive process that relies on general knowledge, reference to the immediate context, and reference back to earlier parts of the game or story. They suggest that children mentally "flag" the props in a pretend game, to rk, for example, the block as a pig. These flags are edited as the game proceeds, for example, the pig gets wet if tea is poured on it. And the flags are read when some action is required, for example, the pig needs to be dried. The crucial question, which Henry Wellman and Anne Hickling raise in their commentary, is this: do children see the "flags" as being in the world or in the mind?[20] That is, do they assume that someone who arrives after the game has begun knows what has been stipulated as what—that the block is a pig, for example— and expect that person to be able to play along in the game? Only further research will answer this question.

On any account, it is clear that from a very young age, children do engage in pretend play with enjoyment and some understanding. They can keep track of what is real and what is pretend. They know the cloth isn't really a pillow, the banana not really a telephone. They keep pretense and reality separate. They don't confuse thoughts and things.

Distinguishing between Thoughts and Things

According to Henry Wellman, this distinction between thoughts and things is the bedrock on which the child's theory of mind is built.[21] One feature of a theory, he says, is that it makes ontological distinctions; that is to say, it determines what categories or kinds of things exist. The basic category distinction a theory of mind makes is that between the world and the mind, between the real world "out there" and the mental world. In our everyday lives we are all "commonsense realists" in this sense.[22] We all believe there is a real world that exists independent of our thoughts about it, and further, we believe we do have thoughts about that world. We understand that our thoughts are private, that they cannot be seen or touched, and that sometimes, as mental images for example, they can be made to come and go at will. Things, on the other hand, can be seen and touched. They have a public and often consistent existence. The table and chairs in the room can be seen and touched by anyone who enters, and they are there from one day to the next. Do young children have such understanding? Do they make these same distinctions between thoughts and things? As we saw in Chapter 1, Piaget thought they didn't; he said, "The child cannot distinguish a real house, for example, from the concept or mental image or name of the house."[23] Henry Wellman disputes this claim. He and his colleagues conducted a series of experiments that demonstrate how sophisticated preschoolers' understanding of the distinction between thoughts and things really is.

These studies clearly show that children between three and five years of age can distinguish between real things and mental entities, such as thoughts, memories, dreams, and pretenses. The children were shown pictures of a boy who had a cookie, for example, and a boy who was thinking about a cookie, or dreaming of one, remembering one, or pretending to have one. Even the three-year-olds could say which boy could see, touch, eat, or let his friend eat the cookie, and they could also say that the first boy's cookie was real and the second boy's cookie was not real. In these experiments the children were also able to distinguish between thoughts and potentially more confusing real things such as smoke, sounds, and photographs. In one of the studies, three-year-olds could distinguish between an object, such as a cup, a mental image of a cup, and a real cup hidden in a box. They knew they could touch the cup on the table in front of them and see it with their eyes, but not the one in the box or the one "in their head." And they understood that they could transform the image but not the real object, just by thinking about it (for example, they could turn the cup upside down). Further, they were able to give explanations to justify these judgments. They said they couldn't touch the image because "it's not real" or "because it's my imagination," whereas they said they couldn't touch the hidden cup because it was in the box.

It seems clear from Wellman's experiments that children do make the same basic distinction we do between thoughts and things. Why did Piaget find otherwise? Wellman says it was because Piaget asked general questions about abstract mental entities rather than simple, direct questions about specific mental entities like those in his studies. Moreover, his technique compared children's judgments of mental entities and real things, whereas Piaget relied solely on children's ability to produce verbal explanations of only mental phenomena, and he interpreted children's figurative explanations, that dreams are pictures, for example, too literally. The child may have meant that dreams are like pictures.

Remember the earlier discussion about the two discoveries the child has to make about the mind: what it is and what it does. Wellman's findings are relevant to the first of these. Conceivably, children could answer questions about mental entities without understanding that the mind represents, without understanding that it is the mind that constructs these entities. According to Josef Perner, three-year-olds' ability to distinguish between real and mental entities depends only on their understanding the content of their images, thoughts, memory, and so on, as "imagined situations."[24] They do not understand that their mental images, thoughts, and memories are representations produced by the mind. Wellman also agrees that, although three-year-olds can distinguish mental entities from real things, they do not understand that the mental things are constructed by the mind.

Although three-year-olds perform so well on these

experimental tasks, the boundary between reality and fantasy may still not be clearly drawn for them, as this sample of dialogue illustrates:

> Pretend there's a monster coming, OK?
> No, let's don't pretend that.
> OK, why?
> 'Cause it's too scary, that's why.[25]

Anyone who has given a home to a preschooler's imaginary friend, and John and Elizabeth Newson's work[26] suggests that this includes at least a quarter of all parents, will recognize that reality and imagination are not always kept strictly apart in the young child's world. As I said earlier, in contrast to real things, mental entities cannot be seen and touched and do not have a consistent and public existence. But an imaginary friend is a consistent character who may be part of the child's life for months, even years. The friend may also acquire a "public existence," at least within the family, and though he or she is invisible and intangible, allowances must still be made. One mother interviewed by the Newsons, talking about her four-year-old's imaginary friend Janet, said, "We can be watching television, and if my lad sits too close, it's 'You're squashing her [Janet]—get off!' And he has to get off, and all! I think we've all got used to Janet now."[27] It seems as though young children's imaginary friends and companions are quite real to them. As another mother said about her four-year-old son, "I think he can really see this dog [her son's imaginary companion]. In fact, I said to my husband, I think I can see this dog!"[28] And certainly, all those of us whose sleep has been broken by children's fears of imagined ghosts and monsters will wonder how clear children are about the boundary between the real and the fantastic.

Paul Harris wondered the same thing.[29] He thought that preschoolers who were clear about the difference between a real cup and an imagined cup might still not be clear about the unreal status of an imagined monster. He and his colleagues asked four- and six-year-olds to imagine things like "a monster that wags its tail and comes chasing after you." He found that the children were just as well able to say that it wasn't real as they were to say that an imagined cup wasn't real. Even children who admitted to being scared of the creature still acknowledged that it wasn't real. In a further experiment, Harris asked the children to pretend there was a friendly puppy in one box and a scary monster in another box, each of which had a little hole in the side. Even though they knew it was a pretend game, they were more likely to choose to put their finger through the hole in the puppy's box and a stick through the hole in the monster's box. Harris concludes that his experiments "suggest that children systematically distinguish fantasy from reality, but are tempted to believe in the existence of what they have merely imagined."[30] Perhaps we ourselves are not so different. I cry real tears at the theater, and sometimes I feel real fear when I lie in bed reading late at night. Just imagination—yes. Young children know that too, though they may be less skillful at reminding themselves of it and comforting themselves with the thought.

Nonetheless, young children really do know the difference between the representation and reality, between thoughts and things. They know that thoughts are "just in your head." They know the thought-of cookie cannot be shared with your friends. However, the thought of a cookie can be shared. It can be shared in language. The next chapter will look at how thoughts are shared and then at how, knowing other people's thoughts, we can predict and explain their actions.

5 / Thought and Language

As we have seen, young children are clear about the difference between thoughts and things. They are able to explain that a boy who is just thinking about a cookie can't see it or touch it or share it with his friends, because it isn't real, it is just in his head. Why "just in his head"? Our commonsense understanding of mind assumes that mental activity goes on in the brain (at least our twentieth-century Western common sense does), and it appears that quite young children have some understanding of the functions of the brain and its location in the head. In an experimental study, some four-year-olds and most five-year-olds judged that, just as you need your hands to tie your shoes, so you need your brain to think and to dream and to remember, and they told the examiner that his brain was in his head, and that a doll didn't have a brain.[1]

We believe that mental states, such as thinking and remembering, originate in the brain. Mental states are brain states caused by particular patterns of activated neurons. Some philosophers and psychologists then argue, as I mentioned in Chapter 1, that if mental states are simply brain states scientific psychology has no need for them. Mental state concepts are like concepts of ghosts and fairies, which are part of our folklore, or like concepts of phlogiston and ether, which are part of an earlier but now disproven theory. Thus, concepts of thoughts and wants, of beliefs and desires should be left where they belong, in folk psychology. That is their proper place; a scientific explanation of human action does not require them.

Mental States

Nonetheless, as I said in Chapter 2, other philosophers and psychologists do regard mental states, such as beliefs and desires, as real states.[2] They do not deny that such states are brain states. They do not claim that the mind exists *independent* of the brain, as a dualist would. They do not say, as Descartes once did, that mind and matter, the psychological and the physical, are independent of each other. What they do argue is that the mind is *not* the brain and that we can think about mental states without reducing them to brain states, just as we can think of animals and plants without reducing them to chemicals. Although our bodies and those of other animals are composed of chemical substances organized in particular ways, we do not think zoologists are wasting their time describing different animal species and their characteristics. That is, we do not suggest that all zoology should be reduced to chemistry, even though we acknowledge that some chemical composition underlies the animal body. In just the same way we can acknowledge that the brain underlies the mind but still talk about organization at the mental level. According to this view, beliefs and desires are mental phenomena; they function in explanations at the mental level. We can explain and predict people's behavior by appealing to this mental level in a way that we cannot do by appealing to brain states, at least at the present time.

The question then becomes, How do we characterize this mental level? As we saw in Chapter 2, Brentano claimed that intentionality (in its technical, philosophical sense) is the mark of the mental, is what distinguishes the mental level from the physical realm. Intentionality is *aboutness*—mental or intentional states are always about something. Something in the world is represented in the mind. What does that mean—to be represented in the mind? This is an enormous question, to which I will give only a very partial answer: When I took my coffee mug back to the kitchen this morning I dropped it, it broke, and I swept the pieces into the garbage. But I remember the mug; I can picture it in my mind, I can see the blue flowers on it. Just now I am feeling hungry. I will call and order a pizza; I think of a list of things I want on the pizza—double cheese, peppers, no olives. When I think about the mug and the pizza, they are things that exist in the world, or at least they *did* or *could* exist. Thinking about things, we present them to ourselves in our mind. Perhaps we present them to ourselves in pictures or in words but perhaps not. Nevertheless, in some way, when we think we re-present the world in mind. Our mental states are thus re-presentations.

We can have any number of different representations: I remember the mug; I want a pizza. We represent not just objects but events and states of affairs too: I remember my mother gave me that mug; I want the pizza delivered to my house. "My mother gave me the mug" and "The pizza will be delivered to my house" are statements, or what are called *propositions*. Thus, mental states are often described as *attitudes* to propositions. They consist of a propositional content to which the person has a certain attitude, such as holding it to be true or wanting it to happen. The attitude denotes what type of mental state it is—belief, desire, and so on—and the content what it is about. For example:

Attitude Type of mental state	Proposition Content, what it is about
believe	(there are olives on the pizza)
desire	(peppers on the pizza)
intend	(call the pizza place)

We can hold different attitudes to the same proposition, resulting in quite different mental states. I can *believe* the pizza will arrive in five minutes, *want* the pizza to arrive in five minutes, *hope* it will arrive in five minutes, and so on. There is obviously a difference between believing something to be true and wanting something to be the case, even when the propositional content of the belief and the desire are the same. Beliefs are caused by things in the world—we see something or are told something and therefore come to hold certain beliefs about it. For example, the pizza comes and we see olives on it. The relationship between a belief and reality is characterized by truth (or falsity). That is, if the propositional content of my belief corresponds to the way things actually are in the world, then the belief is true. If it does not correspond, then it is false. If it is false, I can make it true by changing the belief. I thought there would be peppers on the pizza but I was wrong, I see olives, not peppers, and so I change my belief.

Desires are different from beliefs because they are neither true nor false. The relationship between a desire and reality is one of fulfillment (or unfulfillment). If the propositional content of my desire corresponds to the way things actually are in the world, then my desire is fulfilled. If the desire is not fulfilled, I cannot fulfill it by changing the desire. I wanted peppers on the pizza but there are olives; in order to fulfill my desire I must send it back to be exchanged for one with peppers. Things in the world have to change in order to fulfill the desire. Indeed, our desires may cause changes in the world by leading to intentions that determine actions that bring about change. Intentions, too, are neither true nor false. Like desires, their relationship to the world is one of fulfillment or unfulfillment. If the content of my intention does not match the way the world is, I can fulfill the intention by acting to change things in the world.

In contrast, emotions are not true or false, nor are they fulfilled or unfulfilled. Emotions don't relate to the world in either of these ways. If I am angry that the pizza place got my order wrong, then my anger presupposes a belief that they got my order wrong, but the anger isn't *true* in the way the belief is. Or if I'm happy the pizza's got peppers on it (I don't know yet that it hasn't) then my happiness presupposes a belief that the pizza does indeed have peppers on it, but the happiness isn't *false* in the way the belief is.

This is putting it all very simply, perhaps too simply. Beliefs are not just true or false, but are held with varying degrees of certainty (*convictions, opinions, skepticism*). A belief may be about the past or the future (*memories* or *expectations*). Desires may vary in strength (*wishes, needs, longings*). So may intentions and emotions (*resolution* or *proposal, bliss* or *satisfaction*). Beliefs are not just caused by things in the world, but what we already believe (or desire) may color our interpretation of events in the world and partly determine our new beliefs. Similarly, we may sometimes decide that we desire what the world has served up to us unchosen. Belief and desire may combine, as in *hope*. And so on, and so on—there are thousands of terms referring to mental states and numerous classifications of them.³ Nonetheless, underlying all this variety and subtlety, these are the mental states that are "just in our heads."

Speech Acts

We have seen that even three-year-olds know that the cookie (or the pizza) which is just in your head cannot really be shared with your friend. But if the thought-of pizza can't be shared, the thought of a pizza can be. Our thoughts are shared in language. We don't use language just to share our thoughts, just to convey our beliefs to others, we also use language to make things happen, to realize our desires. I call the pizza place and give my order. The order is an expression of my desire. As I said in Chapter 3, human interaction is essentially an interaction of minds, of mental states: people have beliefs about others' wants, desires to make others believe something, beliefs that others intend to do something, desires to make others believe they intend to do something, and so on. However, as I also said, this social interaction does not proceed directly via the interaction of mental states, it proceeds indirectly, by way of language. Mental states are expressed in *speech acts*, which are the basic units of communication.⁴

Speech acts are things we do with words, to use J. L. Austin's neat phrase,⁵ such as making statements, asking questions, giving orders, making promises, expressing thanks, and so on. Like mental states, speech acts consist of attitudes to propositions. However, the attitude is usually referred to as the *force* of the speech act. The force is how we want the proposition to be taken by the hearer, that is, as a statement, or a request, or a promise. We may indicate the force explicitly using a speech act verb, as in

"I *assure* you those cookies are stale," "I *ask* you to buy me some cookies," "I *promise* to share them with you." But force may be communicated simply by gesture and intonation. For example, depending on the circumstances, the one-year-old's "Cookie!" may mean 'that's a cookie' or 'give me a cookie.' Alternatively, the force may be marked by the type of sentence used. For example, statements are often expressed as declaratives—"Those cookies look good." Questions are expressed as interrogatives—"Are there any cookies?" and orders or requests as imperatives—"Give me a cookie (please)!" However, there is no necessary connection between the type of speech act and the type of sentence. "Those cookies look good" or "Are there any cookies?" might also function as requests in the right circumstances, as indeed might "I'm hungry."

Just as we can hold different attitudes to the same proposition, resulting in different mental states, so we can express the same proposition with different forces, resulting in different speech acts. For example, we can make a statement: "There are peppers on the pizza." We can make a request: "May I have peppers on the pizza?" We can make an apology: "I'm sorry there are peppers on the pizza." More important, a mental state and a speech act may have the *same* propositional content. For example, you believe there are some cookies in the cupboard and you say, "There are some cookies in the cupboard"; the statement expresses the belief that there are cookies in the cupboard. And just as the belief is true if there are cookies in the cupboard and false if there aren't, so too the statement is true if there are cookies there and false if there aren't. In a similar way, the speech act of requesting expresses the mental state of desire, and the speech act of promising expresses the mental state of intention. "I ask you to buy me some cookies," expresses my desire that you to buy me some cookies. "I promise to share them," expresses my intention to give you some.

Thus, the performance of any speech act is necessarily an expression of the corresponding mental state. It would be paradoxical to state a proposition and then deny belief in that proposition: "It's raining and I don't believe it's raining." This is Moore's paradox. However, you don't necessarily have the belief that you have expressed. You may say "There are some cookies in the cupboard," knowing full well there aren't, because you don't want to go to the store. Nonetheless, the belief you don't have has necessarily been expressed in your statement. Similarly, I can say "I promise to share them with you" knowing full well I plan to eat them all myself, yet the intention to share them has necessarily been expressed in my promise. Lies and false promises, though common enough, are deviant. They allow us to conceal our mental states when we don't want to reveal what is really in our minds. Language works as a way of sharing our mental states, however, because most of the time our statements express our beliefs, our requests express our desires, our promises express our intentions. Human interaction is this interaction of minds, mediated by language. Learning what is in people's minds from their language enables us to predict and explain their actions.

Thoughts, Words, and Deeds

Do you remember Carl, who raced past me in the first chapter without stopping to talk? It was because he thought he was late and he wanted to get to his meeting on time. Such a folk psychological explanation, I said, is produced by a theory of mind, which appeals to unseen mental states in order to predict and explain what people do. If we know that Carl thinks he is late and that he wants to be on time, we can predict that he will hurry past us. But how do we know he thinks he is late? If we see him race by and we know he wants to get to the meeting on time, we explain his action by saying he must think he is late—we infer the mental state from the action. If he rushes by, crying, "I mustn't be late!," we know he wants to be on time—we infer the mental state from words, from his speech acts.

We have to distinguish three things: thoughts, words, and deeds. *Thoughts* are the mental states, the beliefs, desires, intentions, and emotions that guide and motivate behavior. *Words* are the expression of those mental states in speech acts—beliefs as assertions, desires as requests, intentions as promises, regrets as apologies, gratitude as thanks, and so on. *Deeds* are the behavior itself, people's actions and interactions that our folk psychology attempts to predict and explain. The mental states are unseen, we see only the actions and hear the speech acts. We infer the mental states from their expression in language and behavior.

We can infer the intention from the action. Margaret Donaldson has said that this is an important way in which children make sense of the world.[6] Moreover, if what someone has said does not accord with the interpretation a young child has given to the action, the child disregards what was said. Children don't interpret the words in isolation, they interpret situations, sometimes without understanding the words (remember the Arab boy at the end of Chapter 3). Thus, for young children, "actions speak louder than words." Their awarenesss of other people's mental states is an awareness of those states expressed in action, not in language. Indeed, for all of us, actions sometimes speak louder than words. However, we are aware of the independent role of the speech act, distinct from mental states and actions, and as children get older they also become more aware of it.[7]

Predicting and Explaining Human Action

As I have said, we are folk psychologists. We want to know why people did what they did and we wonder what they are going to do. We predict and explain their actions from their mental states, we infer mental states from their speech acts and from their actions. There are always three basic considerations: belief, desire, and action. Given any two of these we can infer the third. We can think of these three as core concepts within the theory of mind (see *Figure 1*).

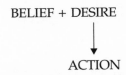

Figure 1. Core concepts within the theory of mind.

In the next three chapters I will look at children's understanding of these concepts. Can young children use knowledge of someone's beliefs and desires to predict his actions? Can they explain what someone does in terms of what she thinks and wants? When do children acquire these core concepts? Before answering such questions we need to see how this triad fits into the larger theory.

Beliefs reflect the way the world is, or at least the way we take it to be. Thus, if we discover we are wrong, we change our belief to fit the way things actually are in the world. How do we discover this? Generally through perception: wrong beliefs are corrected and new beliefs

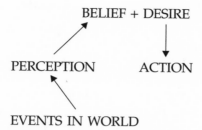

BELIEF + DESIRE

PERCEPTION   ACTION

EVENTS IN WORLD

Figure 2. Information acquired from the world.

are formed because of things in the world, objects and events, that we see or are told about. Sometimes this happens directly and sometimes indirectly, through inference for example. My neighbor goes to work in her car or on the bus. Yesterday I saw her driving by and so I knew she had gone by car. This morning I can see her car in her driveway and so I infer that today she has gone by bus. In general then, belief-type states are concerned with information acquired from the world, what Josef Perner refers to as "getting it in"[8] (see *Figure 2*).

Desires, on the other hand, are concerned with "getting it out." They reflect the way we want the world to be, that is, outcomes we would like to see, and they may cause change in the world because they motivate us to act in order to bring about those outcomes. It is not our mind that has to change, it is the world that has to change to fit our desire. We may not act on all of our desires, for indeed we may entertain conflicting desires and thus it would be impossible to satisfy all of them. However, in order to satisfy a particular desire we may form an intention to act that may lead to action; "may" because just as not all of our desires are satisfied, so not all of our intentions will be fulfilled. We could say that intention is produced from desire and belief, essentially by incorporating a belief about how the desire may be satisfied. I want a new shirt for Saturday's party and I believe I can get one at a store downtown, thus I intend to go downtown. In addition, just as new beliefs are inferred from existing beliefs and perceptions, such as my belief that my neighbor has gone to work on the bus, so new desires are formed from existing desires and intentions: Now I want to leave work early this afternoon so I can go downtown.

It is important to notice how intentions differ from desires. They come from desires and, like desires, they are not true or false but are fulfilled or not by outcomes in the world. Also, like desires, intentions bring about changes in the world. However, desires are fulfilled just so long as the desired outcome is achieved, it doesn't matter how. If I want to have a new shirt for Saturday's party, I might go out and buy one or my sister might happen to visit, bringing me a shirt she has bought that doesn't fit her. Either way, my desire is satisfied (provided I approve my sister's choice, of course). But if I intend to buy a new shirt, then my intention is not carried out unless I go downtown and buy one. That is to say, the outcome of an intention must be achieved as a result of the intention and the actions it causes, and not in any other way. This is the crucial feature that distinguishes intentions from desires; the intention must cause the action that achieves the outcome.[9] In either case, these outcomes, sometimes resulting from our own actions and sometimes not, are perceived as events in the world and thus lead to new beliefs (see *Figure 3*).

Beliefs and desires, then, relate to the world through perception and intention. Carl saw the clock and knew it was late. He wanted to be on time and so he intended to hurry. Is this the whole story? Beliefs come, as it were, from the world via perception. But where do desires

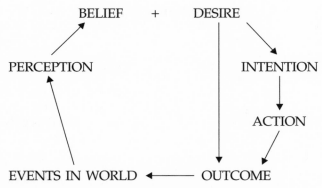

Figure 3. Desires and intentions are satisfied by outcomes in the world.

come from? They come from basic emotions and needs, and ultimately from basic physiological drives, to survive and reproduce. If Carl is late again he will lose his job, and if he loses his job he will have no income and won't be able to eat or support his family.

Desires also come from more cognitive emotions, so-called because they are products of cognition. For example, Carl wants to be a good employee, he believes he should be punctual, he knows he has been late every week, and he is ashamed of that. His shame is produced by his past beliefs and desires and it fuels his current desire to be on time. Many emotions have this dual nature; they are produced from beliefs and desires and they lead to further desires. For example, just now I was hungry, I wanted (desire) a piece of cake with my coffee, I thought (belief) there was some left in the refrigerator, I went to get it and discovered that someone had eaten the last piece. I was surprised (emotion) that my belief was wrong, sorry (emotion) that my desire was unsatisfied, and I want (desire) to go out and buy some more.

This then, is the theory of mind, in bare outline (see

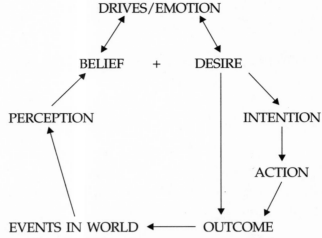

Figure 4. The theory of mind.

Figure 4). Desires come from basic drives and emotions that are part of our biological nature, and from other emotions that are products of belief and desire. Desires may lead to intentions and actions, resulting in outcomes that are events in the world. Desires may also be satisfied by events that just happen, that are not a result of our own actions. Beliefs come from our perception of these events and other happenings in the world, sometimes directly and sometimes indirectly through inference. Needless to say, adults' theory of mind is considerably more detailed and complicated than this outline suggests,[10] but this is sufficient for our present purpose, which is to look at children's understanding.

6 / Thinking about Wanting

Our actions are produced by our desires and our beliefs in combination. If we look for something (action) in a particular place, we must want it (desire) and think we can find it there (belief). Paul Harris's metaphor makes this very clear: "desires . . . provide a direction for our behavior, whereas beliefs provide a map with which progress in the desired direction may be assessed."[1] And so, to understand people's actions, we have to know what their map is and which direction they are headed in, that is, we have to take both their beliefs and their desires into account. Nonetheless, insofar as it is possible to consider the understanding of belief without desire, and of desire without belief, in this chapter I will focus on children's understanding of desire, intention, and emotion. (Their understanding of perception, knowledge, and belief and will be taken up in Chapters 7 and 8.)

Talking about Desire and Emotion

We talk more about our desires and emotions than we do about our beliefs and perceptions, at least we talk about them more explicitly *as* desires and emotions. We say we *want* this and we *feel* that. We also talk about beliefs and perceptions, it's true. We say we *think* this and we *see* that. Much of the time, however, we don't talk about our beliefs and perceptions *as* beliefs and perceptions, we simply take them as the way the world is. Since we all live in the same world we assume we share the same beliefs and perceptions. I could say, "I see my neighbor's car in the driveway, I think she must have gone to work on the bus," but I am more likely to say, "There's her car in the driveway, she must have gone to work on the bus." I report these things as being out there in the world, not as being in my mind, and I assume they are out there for you too. You have the same perceptions and can make the same inferences. Of course I can talk about my beliefs if I have to. For example, if I make a mistake I can refer to what I used to believe, "I thought it was her car but it's not." And if we disagree I can acknowledge that you think one thing and I think something else. Nevertheless we assume that because we live in the same world we share a common set of basic beliefs. Indeed, if we didn't it would be impossible for us to communicate with one another or understand one another's behavior.[2]

It might seem that we share the same basic desires too. However, perhaps what we share are the same beliefs about what is desirable—survival, for example—but I want *me* to survive and you want *you* to survive. Our desires and emotions are personal, uniquely ours. They aren't out there in the world. Even though we live in the same world, I can't assume that we feel and want the same things. We look out of the window and we both see that it is raining. I can be pretty sure you have a belief that it is raining, just as I do. In fact, I don't even think of these as beliefs—it's just raining out there and both of us have to go out in it. However, I can't assume that we have the same feelings and desires about it. I'm happy it's raining—now I won't have to water my flowers. I want it to keep on raining—the garden is dry after all that sun. You are not at all happy it's raining—you're going to the ballgame and you want the rain to stop. These feelings and desires are in our own minds; they are uniquely ours. Our perceptions and beliefs about the rain are in our minds too, but because they are shared, they are somehow out there in the world. This suggests the question, If we did share the same desires, would we assume that they were out in the world, that desirability was a feature of the situation, as it were? Sometimes perhaps we do, but we are well aware of the subjectivity of desire when we need to be; beauty lies in the eye of the beholder, after all.

For these reasons, then, it is not surprising that we talk more explicitly about desires and emotions than about beliefs. It is also not surprising that children start to talk about what people want and feel before they talk about people's beliefs. Karen Bartsch and Henry Wellman examined samples of the everyday speech of ten children from before they were two years old until they were five.[3] Slightly more than 200,000 utterances were searched for examples of terms expressing desire or belief, such as *want, wish, hope, afraid, think, know, expect, understand.* Terms like these were included in about 6 percent of the samples, so their analysis is based on more than 12,000 uses of these desire/belief terms. The first desire term children use is *want:* it comprises 97 percent of all the desire expressions in the data. This will come as no surprise to parents of young children who all day hear, "I want this," "I want that," "I don't want to," and so on.

Bartsch and Wellman weren't interested merely in *which* particular words children use, which may not tell us much about what they understand about the mind, rather they were interested in *how* these words were used. They distinguished instances of genuine reference to the mind, what they called psychological use of the terms, from other uses. In Chapter 3 we saw how babies begin to communicate, first with gestures and then with words. I said they might use a grasping gesture as a request for something, later name it, and by two years say they "want" it. Many toddlers say "Want juice" or "Want cookie." But this may be no more than a request, something like saying "Give me juice." The toddler may have no awareness of the psychological state of desire. However, Bartsch and Wellman found that genuine reference to the subjective mental state of desire occurred around two years of age, much earlier than reference to beliefs, and that children referred to other people's desires as well as their own. For example, "Here [offers object]. That OK? You want that?" and "Fraser [someone else] wants more coffee."[4] Bartsch and Wellman also identified times when the child made an explicit contrast between his or her own psychological state and that of another person, for example, "Do you want me to look both ways? I don't wanna look both ways."[5] Even two-year-olds can make explicit distinctions between their own and others' desires. I suppose parents of Terrible Twos don't need to be told that.

Two-year-olds also talk about feelings, again, both their own and those of other people. As we saw in Chapter 3, even babies recognize different facial expressions of emotion. By the time they are two, children have started to use words to describe these emotions, and this vocabulary increases remarkably during their third year.[6] Most two-year-olds know words for the six universal basic emotions discussed in Chapter 2.

- Happiness: Santa will be *happy* if I pee in the potty.

- Sadness: You *sad*, Daddy?
- Fear: Bees everywhere. *Scared* me!
- Anger: Don't be *mad*, Mommy!
- Surprise: Daddy *surprised* me.
- Disgust: Taste *yucky*, Mom!

These examples come from a study of thirty children who were two years and four months old at the time the samples were collected.[7] The children not only knew these words, they also understood something about the links, described in the previous chapter, between events, emotions, and action. They talked about how things that happened caused a particular emotion, for example:

- I give a hug. Baby be happy.
- It's dark. I'm scared.
- Grandma mad. I wrote on wall.

They recognized that if someone felt a certain way, there must be some reason for it, and they could ask about that:

- You sad, Mommy? What Daddy do?

And they realized that you can tell something about how people feel from how they look or how they behave:

- Katie not happy face. Katie sad.
- I not cry now, I happy.

How do children come to understand these links? How do they know what the causes and consequences of different emotions are? One way may be from participating in family talk. Judy Dunn and her colleagues have shown that children who heard more talk about feelings at eighteen months talked more about feelings at two years of age.[8] Children's participation in such family conversations presumably promotes their understanding of different emotions, and of other people's experience of emotion as well as their own. It has been suggested that children use emotion terms to refer first to themselves, then to the visible features of others' emotions, and lastly to emotions that they infer in others.[9] In contrast, Wellman and his colleagues have found that from a very young age children refer to both their own and others' emotions.[10] Maybe young children *can* talk about others' feelings, but, like many of us, they talk more about their own. And they do seem aware of the importance of the face in displaying how we feel: as Katie, at three, said to her mother, "Look what you've done to my face, you made it sad!"

Young children get a lot of practice at making inferences about emotions in their pretend play. Many observers of young children's make-believe games have noticed how children can put on a pretend emotion from a pretend cause and play out its pretend consequences. For example, Katie and her two-year-old friend Sarah were having a pretend picnic in the living room:

Katie: There's a monster coming!

Sarah: Ohh . . .

Katie: We're scared!

Sarah: We're scared!

Katie: Let's hide.
(Both children ran out into the hall)

Young children also ascribe emotions to dolls and other toy figures. For example, one child made a girl doll take a toy bear from a boy doll, saying, "She took the boy's bear and he's sad."[11] This example comes from a study in which nine children were observed from the time they were one year old until they were seven. All the children first ascribed speech and action to dolls, then they ascribed perceptions and sensations, then emotions and obligations, and last cognitions. Although all the children followed this same order, there was variation in the age at which they first made these different kinds of ascriptions. For example, the children ascribed emotions to dolls during their third year, the first child not long after his second birthday and the last child just before her third. Also, even though all the children could make all these different kinds of ascription by the time they were four years old, there was variation in the ones they used most. Some children were more likely to focus on the talk and action between the characters, whereas others were more likely to describe their characters' internal feelings. In general the boys focused on action and the girls on feelings, although we cannot make too much of this because there were only three boys and six girls in the study. In addition, all the children could make all the ascriptions, so the observed differences are ones of preference rather than ability.

However, people certainly do differ in the extent to which they talk about emotions, and these differences may be associated with gender. In Judy Dunn's study, just mentioned, where children who heard more talk about feelings at eighteen months talked more about feelings at two years, Dunn found that mothers and older siblings talked more about feelings to girls than to boys at eighteen months, and that by two years of age the girls talked more about feelings than the boys did. What might the consequences of such individual differences be? Dunn and her colleagues wondered whether children who grow up in families where there is a lot of talk about feelings are any better at understanding other people's emotions later on.[12] They had observed children at home around the time of their third birthday and had a record of how much the children, their mothers, and their siblings had talked about feelings and in what contexts. When the children were six-and-a-half years old they were given a test of their ability to identify other people's feelings. They listened to tape-recorded conversations between a man and a woman whom they didn't know. In the conversations one person's feeling changed, for example from happy to sad, and the children were asked to say how that person had been feeling at the beginning and how he or she felt at the end. Dunn and her colleagues found that the children who performed best on this task were the ones who had grown up in families where there was a lot of talk about emotion. This didn't depend on how verbally fluent the children were nor on how much total talk there was in the family, and interestingly, in this study no gender differences were found.

Dunn's study is noteworthy because it shows a connection between what was found when children were observed in their homes at one age and their performance in an experimental situation some time later. In Chapter 1 I mentioned the ongoing debate over the best way to find out about children's understanding of the mind. Should we just watch children in everyday situations and listen to what they say, or should we try to control the situation in an experimental investigation? Do these different methods yield similar or conflicting results?

Experiments Investigating Understanding of Desires and Emotions

Sometimes it is hard to know whether we are reading too much into what a young child says. Does she really understand what it means or is she just repeating something she has heard someone else say in a similar situation? This is one reason psychologists turn to experimentation. In an experiment we have more control over what happens: We can describe a scenario to the child and ask her about it. We can describe it in the same way to many children of different ages and see how they answer. The disadvantage, of course, is that the story we tell is not part of the child's life. Her thoughts and feelings aren't involved in the way they are when she's interacting with family and friends. And if the experimental situation itself is strange to the child, it might mask understanding she really does possess. However, even very young children are so used to listening to stories and talking about them, they readily fall into answering an experimenter's questions about them, especially when the experimenter has taken time to get to know the children and make them feel comfortable. In the case of children's understanding of desires and emotions we find remarkable congruence between the observational and the experimental data.

We have just seen that two-year-olds talk about desires, about what they want and what other people want. Experiments show that two-year-olds understand that people act to satisfy their desires, that is, a person who wants something will do something to try to get it. For example, Henry Wellman and his colleagues told children stories in which a boy wanted to find something, such as his rabbit, to take to school.[13] They were told the rabbit might be hiding in the garage or under the porch. There were cutout pictures of the boy and the hiding places so the story could be acted out for the child to help her understand it. The boy then looked in one of these places, say the garage, and there he found the rabbit (in other versions of the story he found his dog or he found nothing). Then the children were asked what the boy would do next: Would he look under the porch or would he go to school? These young children knew that in the first case, in which he has found the rabbit, he would go to school, and that in the other two cases he would go and look under the porch. Of course the same child didn't hear all three versions of one story, that would be too confusing, but she heard other stories with a similar structure and different content. From these results we can see that even two-year-old children understand the connection between desires and outcomes, and recognize that an unsatisfied desire leads to further action.

The children were also told the same stories without hearing why the character wanted to find the desired object, just that he or she wanted it. For example, Linda wants to find her mittens, which may be in the closet or in her backpack. She looks in her backpack and finds them (or in other versions finds nothing there or finds her crayons instead). This time the children were asked about the character's emotional reaction: Does she feel happy or does she feel sad? Once again, two-year-olds were very successful at making appropriate judgments. They said that characters who found what they wanted would be happy and those who found something else or nothing would be sad. This judgment depended appropriately on what they knew the character wanted, and so they judged that a boy who was looking for his rabbit would be sad if he found his dog, whereas a character who was looking for a dog would be happy if he found a dog. That is to say, they did not assume that desirability was a feature of the situation, that everyone would be happy finding a dog.

In all of these stories the characters wanted to find something, that is, the outcomes of their desires were to be achieved by their own action, and so we could perhaps talk equally well here of desires or intentions. In fact we could think of a sort of undifferentiated desire-intention state, which may indeed be the three-year-old view. An understanding of intentions as separate from desires may not develop until later.

Children's Understanding of Intention

We use the notion of intention in two distinct but related ways. We use it to refer to *future planned action,* and we use it to denote *intentional action* in contrast to accidental behavior. Just as two-year-olds talk in the way we do about desires and emotions, they also talk about intentions. From two years on they use some of the same terms we do. We say we *intend to, plan to,* or *are going to* in order to refer to our future actions, and two-year-olds talk about what they are *going to* or *gonna* do. For example two-and-a-half-year-old Alan is sitting on a chair swinging a mop in the air.

Alan: I'm gonna get a fish. (Dips end of mop onto floor, brings it up, turns to caregiver)

Alan: He got a fish, he got a fish, all by myself. . . .

Alan: Eee, ooh! I'm in my boat . . .

Alan: I'm gonna get two fish, fish. (Extends mop and broom over corner of table) A fish![14]

We say we *meant to* do something, or we did it *on purpose* to indicate that a past action was performed deliberately, and we negate these terms to indicate that an action was accidental. Two-year-olds also make these distinctions, for their own actions and those of other people. For example, a two-year-old climbs on his mother to investigate a light switch:

Mother: You're hurting me!

Child: Sorry. Sorry. I don't mean to.[15]

Or a two-year-old comes crying to her mother saying that her brother has bitten her:

Mother: He bit you on the head?

Child: Yes.

Mother to brother: Philip is that true?

Brother: No.

Child to mother: Yes! On purpose![16]

These examples come from Judy Dunn's studies. Dunn says such reference to intentions were not frequently made by the young children she observed, but when they did occur they were completely appropriate. It was Piaget who first said that at three or four years of age a child learns to distinguish between his own deliberate and accidental acts "and soon after this he learns to excuse himself by the plea of 'not on purpose.'"[17] However, it could be that such young children do not really understand the distinction between intentional and unintentional action and use "not on purpose" to get out of trouble. Dunn found no such rote-learned, inappropriate uses in her studies, although parents sometimes report it and examples do exist:

A 3-year-old was helping to feed her baby brother. After spooning in a few mouthfuls of cereal, she took another spoonful and simply dumped it on the baby's head. Then she turned quickly to her very angry mother and claimed, "I didn't do it on purpose."[18]

What might the little girl mean? It is hard to see how you could take a spoonful of cereal and *accidentally* dump it onto someone's head. Perhaps this is just a rote-learned

strategy, said to appease a "very a
haps not. Perhaps, as I've sugg
don't distinguish desires and inte
undifferentiated desire-intention
girl was saying she didn't want it,
that consequence to occur. Even
use the same words we use, we ___
mean what we mean by those words. It might be that
when two- and three-year-olds use the words we use to
refer to intentions, they are talking about undifferentiated desire-intentions. Most of the time what they say
makes perfect sense, because most of the time our desires
and our intentions coincide, and so it's only occasionally
that we find odd examples like the one above. Indeed,
Roger Brown said that when children start to use *gonna,*
wanna, and also *hafta,* at about two years of age, they do
not distinguish between the terms semantically at first
but may have individual preferences for using one rather
than another. The terms "were used to name actions just
about to occur, a kind of immediate future which was
often also a statement of the child's wish or intention,"[19]
(though it presumably need not be, as in "Help! I'm
gonna fall!"). Thus, *want to* (desire) and *going to* (intention) may not be distinguished for the young child. Both
may be used to mark desire-intentions.

Nonetheless, sometimes it is important to think of
intentions as separate from desires. As I said in Chapter
5, intentions are like desires in many ways. We don't fit
our desires and intentions to the world as we fit our
beliefs to the world; rather, it's the world that has to come
to fit our desires and intentions. That is, they are not
mental states that can be true or false, but ones that are
satisfied or not by actions and events in the world. However, although desires and intentions are alike in this
way, there is an important difference between them. De-

e fulfilled so long as the outcome is achieved, it
sn't matter how, but intentions are carried out only
the intention itself causes the action that achieves the
outcome. Remember my new shirt: my *desire* to have a
new shirt was satisfied whether I went to buy one or
took the one my sister brought me, but my *intention* to
buy a new shirt was only carried out by my going out
and buying one. That is to say, in the case of intention,
I myself bring about the outcome, I cause it. This is what
we might call *intentional causation.* When do children
understand this? What does the experimental literature
tell us?

Some time ago, Tom Shultz and his colleagues devised
a number of ingenious tasks to find out how much
young children understand about intention.[20] In one experiment they had the children do certain things, but
sometimes they couldn't help but make a mistake. For
example, Shultz put a dull penny and a shiny penny on
the table and asked the child to point to the shiny one—
easy—except sometimes the child had to wear prism
spectacles that shift left toward right, and so she pointed
to the dull penny by mistake. She was then asked, "Did
you mean to do that?" or a child who was watching was
asked, "Did she mean to do that?" Children as young as
three years of age (the youngest age tested) could, in this
way, distinguish intentional actions from accidental ones,
both for themselves and for other children they observed.

In these tasks the experimenters probably would have
obtained the same result if they had asked, "Did you
want to do that?" Indeed, my colleagues and I have
shown this to be so. We played a game with children to
see if they could remember their desire when it was not
fulfilled.[21] Parents may wonder why one needs an experiment to show this—it is obvious that even toddlers

know what they want, but sometimes, as any parent quickly learns, they can be distracted by an attractive alternative. Do they remember the original desire? As adults, we sometimes tell ourselves we didn't want what we didn't get, the "sour grapes" phenomenon, but we do usually remember what we originally wanted. We found that three-year-olds do too. In our task, if they had said they *wanted to* pick out one particular toy that was hidden in a bag, and they picked out another, equally nice one, they could say they didn't get the one they wanted. In just the same way, if they had said which one they were *going to* pick and they got a different one, they could say they didn't get the one they were *trying to* pick.[22] The language of intention and the language of desire seem indistinguishable in these cases.

In all of these sorts of tasks, such young children may think of desires and intentions indiscriminately, as goal states, and they may succeed by matching goals and outcomes.[23] If the goal and the outcome match, they can say they or another person *wanted* it or *meant to* do it. On the other hand, if there is a mismatch between the goal and the outcome, they can say they didn't want it or didn't mean it. Similarly, in Wellman's stories, described above, the children could succeed by matching goals and outcomes. The children could predict what the story characters would do or how they would feel when they knew what the character wanted and were told what happened. If goal and outcome matched, they could say the character would be happy and would stop searching, and if the two didn't match, they said he would be sad and would carry on looking.

All these judgments of match and mismatch between goal and outcome can be made in the same way for both desire and intention. Children have to compare the hypothetical desired (or intended) situation with the actual

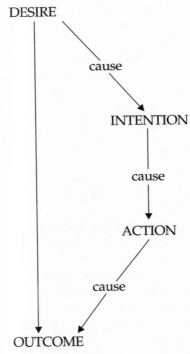

Figure 5. Intentional causation.

situation in the world and judge that the desire (or intention) is fulfilled if the two match, and so the person will be happy, or judge that the desire-intention is unfulfilled if the two do not match, and so the person will be sad. However, it is not clear that because children have the ability to make such judgments they understand intentional causation, that is, that the mind *causes* action.

Desires cause intentions, which cause actions, which cause outcomes. Remember the place of desire and intention in the theory of mind diagram in Chapter 5 (see *Figure 5*).

As Lou Moses has said, it is likely that even very

young children have some introspective notion of the causal power of the mind in producing action.[24] At least, they experience wanting something and doing something to get it. At the same time, they might experience goals as driving their efforts without really understanding the causal nature of intention and its distinction from desire. They might have a simpler concept that does not differentiate between desire and intention (see *Figure 6*).

DESIRE-INTENTION

cause

ACTION/OUTCOME

Figure 6. Desire undifferentiated from intention.

If children can really differentiate between desire and intention they will be able to distinguish between two people who have similar desires, who perform similar actions, and who bring about the same outcome, but only one of whom does so intentionally. The other is involved in what philosophers call a *deviant causal chain*. Here is an example: A man wanted to kill his uncle so that he would inherit a fortune, and one day he was out driving, so wrought up with thinking how he could commit the murder that he accidentally drove over a pedestrian— who happened to be his uncle.[25] Even so, we don't consider this to be an intentional killing. It is a "deviant" causal chain, because, although the man's action caused the outcome and the outcome matched the goal, he still didn't do it on purpose—even though he got what he wanted. The question is, When will children understand such a distinction?

It is hard even to describe such complicated sequences to children, but we can tell them very simple stories in which there is no information about people's goals and so no basis on which to make the match/mismatch comparison. Elizabeth Lee and I told children simple pairs of stories illustrated with pictures.[26] In one an outcome was produced intentionally and in the other the same outcome came about accidentally. We asked the children who meant to produce the outcome. For example, in one story a girl's mother gave her some bread, she took it outside and threw crumbs down on the ground, and birds came and pecked them up. In the other story another girl's mother gave her some bread, she took it outside to eat it, crumbs dropped behind her, and birds came and pecked them up. The children were asked, "Which girl meant the birds to eat the crumbs?" Three-year-olds couldn't tell, but five-year-olds could. That is, the older children could distinguish between intentional and unintentional actions even when they could not look for a match between the actor's goal and the outcome. Why can five-year-olds succeed and not three-year-olds?

In these stories the goal is not explicitly mentioned, so children could not answer correctly by judging the match or mismatch between what the characters wanted and what happened. In order to decide which girl meant the birds to eat the crumbs the children have to realize that in only one case did the girl's desire for the outcome (the birds' eating the crumbs) cause her intention to feed the birds. In other words, they have to understand that the mind is active, that mental activity can bring about events in the world. As I suggested in Chapter 2, at first children may have only a partial understanding of mental representation. They may have some understanding of mental entities, but not of the mind's activity. They may not acquire this more complete understanding of mental representation until the age of four or five. More evidence for this has come from studies of children's understanding of knowledge and belief, the topics of the next two chapters, where I will take this idea up in more detail. However, one last word about desire and intention before we go on to think about knowledge and belief: It has been said that children reach the age of reason at four or five years. Josef Perner, for example, pointed out that children become able to exert some self-control about this time.[27] Perhaps self-control also depends on being able to distinguish between desire and intention: even though you want something you cannot have, you do not intend to do anything to try to get it.

7 / Thinking about Knowing

Emily (three years old):	Grandad! Grandad!
Grandfather:	Yes?
Emily:	We're having a surprise party for your birthday! And it's a secret!
Jeremy (three years old):	Mommy, go out of the kitchen.
Mother:	Why, Jeremy?
Jeremy:	Because I want to take a cookie.[1]

Parents (and developmental psychologists) love to trade anecdotes such as these. We smile as we pass them back and forth among ourselves. But what are we to make of stories like this? As we have just seen, even toddlers understand a great deal about other people's desires and emotions, about what others want and feel. However, there is still a lot they don't understand about other people's thoughts, particularly about what others believe and know. Surprises, secrets, tricks, and lies all depend on understanding and manipulating what others think and know.

As I said at the beginning of Chapter 6, we have to

take both desires and beliefs into account if we are to explain and predict people's actions, or to surprise, tease, comfort, or manipulate them. Usually, however, we focus on what we think people want. We don't think explicitly about their beliefs because, as I said, we live in the same world and share the same set of beliefs. That's true, but we don't share all the same experiences in that world, and even those we do experience together we each experience from a uniquely personal perspective. We thus have to give other people information about our experience and we have to get information from them.

Exchanging Information

Even babies seem to understand, in some simple way, this need to exchange information, or at least they are able to participate in such exchanges. In Chapter 3 I described how a one-year-old can point things out to his mother and will follow his mother's pointing, or even the direction of her gaze, to look where she is looking. Once he can move around he will bring things to show to her and to other people, and once he can talk he will tell them things. Patricia Greenfield gives a nice example of this.[2] She was watching a one-year-old whose mother was occupied teaching a children's gym class. He was whining "shoes, shoes," wanting his mother to put them on for him, but she was busy so Greenfield did it for him. He ran back to his mother, saying "shoes, shoes" again, but this time in an excited voice. He lifted his foot to show her and when she looked at it he pointed to Greenfield. His mother understood and said, "The lady put your shoes on," acknowledging the information he was trying to give her. All of these natural behaviors suggest that, from a very young age, children understand something about how people get to know things—they recognize the role of perception and communication in belief formation.

Perhaps, but again, perhaps not. How much does the one-year-old know as he looks to his mother, points to the woman watching the gym class, and says "shoes"? Does he know that perception causes belief? Does he know that his mother will acquire the same beliefs that he has if she perceives the same things? Does he know that if his mother looks toward where he points she will see the person who put his shoes on? How can we begin to answer these questions? Lab studies show us more precisely what children can do, but even these studies can't always tell us how much children understand about what they do. From the work of Jerome Bruner, George Butterworth, and their colleagues,[3] we know that six-month-olds will turn to look in the direction their mother looks even if they don't fixate on the same object, that by one year they can pick out the object she is looking at, and that by eighteen months they can turn round and look if she gazes at something behind their head. If the mother points to the object while looking at it, the child is even more likely to respond. The baby himself can point where he wants his mother to look, and by about fifteen months he first looks to see that she is looking at him, then points at what has caught his attention, a bright new toy perhaps, and then looks to see if she's looking at it.

This is sophisticated behavior on the part of very young children, and these precise lab studies have given us a lot of information about it. They do not, however, tell us how much we can infer about children's recognition and understanding of what they are doing. For example, does the baby realize that other people see, feel, and think, as she herself does, and is her goal to share those experiences with another person? Some time ago,

Inge Bretherton and her colleagues argued that between nine and twelve months of age the baby recognizes that other people are like herself in psychological as well as in physical ways.[4] That is, babies see that others not only have toes and fingers, noses and mouths, like themselves, but other people, too, have likes and dislikes, can see things and hear things, and can exchange information. Indeed, these researchers were among the first developmentalists to apply Premack and Woodruff's phrase "theory of mind" (see Chapter 1) to human children's understanding of others. They were careful to say that the theory is implicit at first and becomes more explicit in later years. Nonetheless, even their idea of an implicit theory credits babies with an understanding of others as psychological beings.

Similarly, Simon Baron-Cohen has more recently argued that infants' behavior indicates that they understand *attention* as a mental state, which is an important beginning to their understanding of others' minds.[5] He says the fact that babies respond to their mother's pointing and gazing suggests they understand that she directs her attention to interesting objects, and the fact that they check the mother's face when they point suggests they are trying to influence her attention.

Josef Perner, on the other hand, argues that at this stage we don't need to assume that infants are really trying to manipulate their mother's attention in order to share experiences. They may simply be enjoying a newfound ability to manipulate the mother's eye movements.[6] It perhaps seems odd to describe their behavior in this way, since when we ourselves or older children point things out to others, it is obvious that we do so in order to share experiences, to get the other person to look at or talk about something we have seen. Why wouldn't we interpret the infant's behavior in the same way?

Perner argues that babies *are* very different from older children. If we grant too much understanding to infants, we don't leave ourselves room for any interesting explanation of the differences between infants and older children. This is an important theoretical argument. The point here is that infants' behavior itself does not settle the debate. Perhaps we should look at what somewhat older children can do and see whether we would be more willing to attribute an understanding of others' mental states to them.

John Flavell and his colleagues have shown that eighteen-month-old children will respond to requests to show an adult a toy or a picture, and that by the age of two or so they will take care to turn the picture the right way up.[7] Two-year-olds can even succeed on more difficult tasks they are not likely to have learned naturally, such as showing the adult a picture fixed inside the bottom of a small hollow cube. When children first show these pictures, they try to show them in such a way that they can see them at the same time as the adult does, which is quite difficult when the picture is stuck inside a cube. In this case, some of them held the cube low down and tilted it back and forth between themselves and the adult. Perner suggests that eighteen-month-olds show things in this way because they are just coming to an understanding that looking leads to seeing: that looking at a picture leads to a visual experience of it. To assure themselves that the adult sees the picture, they give themselves the same visual experience. Thus, Perner attributes to one-and-a-half to two-year-olds some awareness of others' mental states that he denies to one-year-olds.[8]

There is little experimental work with toddlers, and what there is asks them to do something, as in the showing task. Most of what we know about toddlers' understanding of others comes from observing their talk in everyday situations. However, as we have seen, there are some inherent difficulties in making inferences about children's understanding from observations of their spontaneous behavior and natural language. Even though children may be using the same words we would use, we are not always sure they mean the same things as we would. The child's word meanings are gradually built up. In an experiment, we can arrange the situation in such a way that we know more precisely what children mean by what they say. In addition, in the real world some actions may be learned in a routine way, without much understanding. In an experiment, we can expose children to novel situations which they have to *understand* in order to respond appropriately. For example, very young children may have learned how to show a picture to another person because of their experience in sharing picture books, but they are far less likely to have shown someone a picture stuck in the bottom of a hollow cube, like the one Flavell gave them. The toddlers' success on this task proved that they understood what is required in showing something to another person. Much more experimental work has been done with older preschoolers—three- to five-year-olds. With children this age, as well as asking them to do things we can ask them questions that will allow us, if we are careful to ensure that our meaning is clear, to discover more precisely what they do and do not understand.

Understanding Sources of Knowledge

As such experiments have shown, three-year-olds understand that if an object is hidden in a box, then a person who has looked in the box knows what is in there and someone who hasn't looked doesn't know.[9] Similarly, three-year-olds understand that someone else, sitting in a different place, may see something they can't see from where they are sitting.[10] However, there is still a lot about how we acquire information that three-year-olds don't understand. Even though they understand that the same object can be seen by some people and not by others, they don't understand that people may have different views of the same object. Imagine there is a picture of a turtle on the table between the child and the experimenter. If a screen is placed vertically on the table so that the picture is blocked from one or the other, three-year-olds understand that one person sees it and the other person doesn't. However, without the screen, when they can both look at the turtle, three-year-olds don't understand that one person sees the turtle standing on its feet, while the person at the opposite side of the table sees it lying on its back. By the time they are four, children do understand this.[11]

This illustrates the difference between what John Flavell has called Level 1 and Level 2 understanding. At Level 1 children understand that they or another person may be "cognitively connected" to something, as in seeing versus not seeing it, or knowing about it versus not knowing about it.[12] However, not until Level 2 do children understand something about the mental representations produced by these cognitive connections. This understanding is needed in order to recognize that people may see the same thing in different ways. In the terms that I introduced in Chapter 2, we could say that at Level 1 children have only a partial understanding of representation. They need a more complete understanding of representation, including a notion of *representational activity*, to realize that the mind interprets situations and that different people's minds may produce different interpretations. This is what is achieved at Level 2.

In a similar way, three-year-olds don't understand that, depending on what they already know, different people may get different information from looking at the same thing, but four-year-olds do understand this. In one study, two stuffed animals made of the same gray material, say an elephant and a rabbit, were hidden in separate boxes, each with a little hole in the lid. Only the gray material and nothing else that would identify the animal could be seen through the hole. The experimenter pointed to one box and said, "Do you know it's the elephant in here?" and also asked whether someone else would know. A good number of four-year-olds and most five-year-olds recognize that if you saw the animals being put into the boxes you would know, but if you weren't there and didn't see it, you can't know which animal it is if you see only the gray patch through the hole in the lid.[13] Again, the older children's more sophisticated understanding depends on their recognition that the mind interprets situations and that people may represent the same event differently.

Three-year-olds, indeed even much younger children, certainly know how to acquire information, how to find things out. Yet, as with the one-year-old's communicative abilities, although they know how to do it, it is not clear how much they understand about it. They can obtain information, for instance about what is in a drawer, in different ways—by looking, by feeling, by being told—and they can remember what is in the drawer. But they don't remember how they found this out—they don't remember if they saw it, or felt it, or were told about it—whereas four-year-olds do remember.[14]

Likewise, three-year-olds don't understand that we acquire different information through our different senses: seeing tells us some things and feeling tells us others. If there were two cups on the counter, identical except that one was red and the other blue, and we asked a three-year-old to bring us the red one, she could do it. Similarly, if there were two sponges on the counter, identical except that one was wet and the other dry, and we asked her to bring us the dry one, she could do that too. And doubtless, in the first case she would look at the cups and in the second case she would feel the sponges. Daniela O'Neill and I were intrigued to find that, although they can do these things, three-year-olds don't understand that they have to see something to know its color and feel it to know its texture.[15] If a three-year-old child has been shown two balls, identical except that they are different colors, and if one of the balls is hidden inside a box that the child can either look into or feel inside, she is unable to say what she would have to do (that is, look or feel) in order to be sure which ball is in the box. Later, with John Flavell, O'Neill showed that even if a three-year-old sees one puppet look at the hidden ball and another puppet feel it, she cannot say which puppet knows for sure which ball it is. By age five children can do these things.

All of these experimental studies are concerned with children's understanding of what people know or don't know, and how people can find out things they don't know. Four- and five-year-olds' understanding is quite different from that of two- and three-year-olds. It is not just that four-year-olds have accumulated more experience and knowledge; they also have a different theory about information exchange and knowledge acquisition. They understand what the mind does, that it construes and interprets information, as we will see in the next chapter.

If children really do achieve a new understanding of knowledge at four years of age, we would expect it to be evident in their behavior in everyday life too. Do we see differences between two- and three-year-olds and older children in everyday interactions that might be explained by this change? Consider the game of hide-and-seek: two- and three-year-olds enjoy it just as much as their older siblings do, but do the younger children really understand the point of the game? They enjoy getting out of sight, even though they sometimes don't seem to understand that they must hide their whole body, that not being able to see the seeker doesn't necessarily mean the seeker can't see them. What they most enjoy are the routines of the game, especially when it is played with a cooperative adult, who calls "Where are you?" and looks where you aren't, before the exciting moment of "finding" you.[16] However, three-year-olds seem not to understand what hiding really means, that it involves more than not being seen by the seeker—it involves the seeker's not knowing where you are. As Josef Perner puts it, "These children are quite proficient at getting *out of sight*, they seem not to appreciate that the point of it all is to get *out of knowledge*,"[17] and he tells the story of Heinz Wimmer's son, Theo, at three years of age, playing hide-and-seek with his father. Theo finds Heinz in the pantry, and then he "hides" himself in the pantry, right in front of his father's eyes.

Talking about Thinking and Knowing

We can watch children play, as in hide-and-seek, and try to infer what they understand. However, most often, in making natural observations, we rely on what children say, on how they talk about thinking and knowing. As I mentioned in the previous chapter, children talk about desires and emotions before they talk about beliefs. They also talk early on about what they and others can see and hear. A little girl, two years and three months old, stopped suddenly as she was playing in the garden, cocked her head to one side and said, "Aitopane [aeroplane]. Hear it. Don't see it." Was she aware that we receive information from different modalities, or was she repeating something she had heard someone else say at another time? It is hard for us to know.

The general finding, from Bretherton, Dunn, Wellman, and all those investigating young children's language about internal states, is that children have terms for perception, emotion, and desire before they use words to refer to cognitive states. The first belief terms children use are *think* and *know*. These two words comprised 94 percent of all the belief expressions in Bartsch and Wellman's study (see Chapter 6).[18] Their coding scheme, which examined surrounding utterances for the context of the terms' use, allowed them to distinguish instances of genuine reference to the mind—psychological use of the terms—from mere conversational or uninterpretable uses. A child may use the term *know* in saying "Know what?" to introduce a new topic, a "conversational use" in contrast to "psychological use," which actually refers to someone's knowing, as in "I didn't know you had this. Where did you get it?"[19] Although two-year-olds may use the words *think* and *know,* they do not use these terms for psychological reference, or only rarely and only just before the third birthday. The use of *think* and *know* for psychological reference increases markedly during the fourth year. By four years of age children can explicitly contrast their own beliefs with those of another, for example, "They think they are slimy. I think they are good animals."[20]

Josef Perner emphasizes that young children's use of the terms *know* and *think* is different from that of adults.[21] We use the terms in a variety of ways, only some of which require metarepresentational understanding, that is, understanding that what is known or thought is a representation. Perner argues that before about four years of age children do not use the terms in this meta-representational way. The term *know* picks out three aspects of knowledge. First, knowledge is associated with success: we say we know how to do something, or we know where something is, meaning we can find it. Second, knowledge is associated with truth: we say we know something when what we know corresponds with the facts of the matter in the world. Third, knowledge is formed by exposure to relevant information: we say we know something if we saw it happen. Perner argues that when children first use the term *know,* their primary concern is with successful action: they say they know if they can tell you something or do something correctly. They also use *know* to talk about correspondence with the facts. However, before about four years of age they don't use *know* to talk about the source of their information. They don't talk about how they know something or ask how someone else knows.

When Elliot turned four he started asking people how they knew the things they told him, something he hadn't done previously. For example, his grandmother told him not to throw sand at the pigeons. It would get in their eyes and hurt them. "How do you know that?" he asked.[22] But had Elliot just begun to understand the experimental tasks that assess understanding of sources of knowledge? Systematic study is needed to answer this question, to investigate Perner's suggestions regarding children's use of *know.* It would be especially useful to study children's language development over a period of time and see if they start to talk about the source of their own knowledge and ask about the source of others' knowledge at the same time that they come to perform correctly on the experimental tasks. All we have at the moment are suggestive synchronies from the experimental and observational data, which tell us that at about four years of age, children start to talk about the sources of knowledge and start to perform correctly in source of knowledge experiments.

Similarly and strikingly, in languages where verbs are grammatically marked to indicate the source of one's knowledge, children start to produce the markings correctly at about four years of age. In Turkish the past tense verb is inflected to indicate whether one actually witnessed the event one is reporting, or whether one was told about it or inferred its happening. "The balloon popped [I saw it pop]" would be expressed differently from "The balloon popped [he told me]" or "The balloon popped [I saw the pieces]." Around four years children start to use these inflections correctly and to understand their meanings when they hear them.[23]

Children use the same words we use and, as I've said before, we may not realize that they don't always use them to mean precisely the same things we mean. When three-year-old Katie was brushing her teeth in the bathroom, she took the toothpaste and hid it behind the radiator. She said, "I'm hiding the toothpaste here so Daddy won't find it." We might think she understands, in the same way we do, hiding, finding, seeing, knowing. But does she? Her mother asked, "When Daddy comes into the bathroom, where will he think the toothpaste is?" Katie solemnly pointed to the hidden toothpaste, down behind the radiator. It seems that her understanding is not the same as ours. There is still more to learn about beliefs and false beliefs. That is the topic of the next chapter.

8 / Thinking about Believing

In the previous chapter we saw that from a very young age, children take care to show and tell people things. We saw that their understanding of what it is to know and how one comes to know develops gradually during the preschool years. When Katie was just three years old, she learned how to open the front door on her own to see who was outside on the street. Her mother said to her, "You must tell me when you open the front door. I have to know when you're going outside." The next time Katie went to open the door, she obediently called to her mother, "Are you knowing?" However, it is quite possible to understand that people need to be told or shown something they are unaware of, without understanding that they could have beliefs different from your own. That is, it may be easier to understand that someone does not know something, and so needs to be told or shown it, than to understand that she may hold a false belief—false from your point of view, that is. You think one thing, the door is open, whereas she thinks something else, the door is closed.

As we also saw in the previous chapter, three-year-olds, even two-year-olds, use the word *think*. But as I noted, we have to consider carefully what the child means when he uses a term like *think* or *know*, and whether he is genuinely referring to a mental state. At first children use the word *think* primarily to express uncertainty, as in "I think this is a lamb," which Abe said when he wasn't sure.[1] He could just as well have said, "Maybe it's a lamb." Their other frequent early use of *think* is to introduce an activity, as in "I thoughted we'd eat some cake," which could have been expressed as, "Let's eat some cake."[2] Neither of these uses implies that the child understands that his beliefs are different from someone else's, or even that *think* refers to a mental state. But as Bartsch and Wellman have shown, by the age of four children do use *think* to refer to mental states, even sometimes to express the idea that what they think is different from what somebody else thinks or different from what they themselves used to think.[3]

Understanding False Beliefs

Far more of our knowledge of children's understanding of what other people know and think has come from experimental studies than from naturalistic observation. Indeed, this is where theory of mind work began, in the debate that arose following Premack and Woodruff's claim that the chimpanzee's ability to predict what a human actor will do to achieve certain goals implies that the animal has a theory of mind (see Chapter 1).[4] In this debate, several philosophers suggested a basic test to demonstrate indisputably that someone possesses a theory of mind, the essence of which is this: an individual who has a theory of mind should be able to recognize the consequences of a person's having a false belief.[5]

What people see or what they are told causes them to have beliefs, which inform them about the world. But sometimes people are mistaken about what they have seen, or the situation changes after they have seen it, or someone tells them something wrong. Then their beliefs are false, although they don't know this. People assume that their beliefs are true; indeed, they don't even think of them as beliefs, they just think that's the way the world is (unless or until something happens to correct the belief). So, if someone is mistaken, if he has a false belief, he will act as though his belief were true, that is, he will act on the basis of the mistaken belief. This is the fundamental understanding children need to have in order to perform correctly on false belief tasks. It is the fundamental understanding I referred to in Chapter 2 in discussing mental representation. We can make sense of people's mistaken actions and their reactions of surprise because we understand that people are indirectly related to the world through their mental representation of it. And we understand that they act on the basis of their representations even when the representation does not accurately reflect reality.

When do children understand this? As Daniel Dennett, one of the philosophers who was engaged in this debate, put it:

> Very young children squeal in anticipatory delight as Punch prepares to throw the box over the cliff. Why? Because *they know Punch thinks Judy is still in the box.* They know better; they saw Judy escape when Punch's back was turned. We take the children's excitement as over-whelmingly good evidence that they understand the situation—they understand that Punch is acting on a mistaken belief (although they are not sophisticated enough to put it that way). Would chimpanzees exhibit similar excitement if presented with a similar bit of play acting (in a drama that spoke directly to their "interests")? . . . if they didn't react, the hypothesis that they impute beliefs and desires to others would be dealt a severe blow, even if all the P & W tests turn out positively, just because it

can be made so obvious—obvious enough for four-year-old children—that Punch believes (falsely) that Judy is in the box.[6]

Dennett wrote this (including the prescient comment about four-year-olds) in a plea for direct, natural, plausible tests, and he is right—natural behavior is what matters. However, as I have said before, we need experimental work to help us sort out what inferences we can draw from our observations of natural behavior. It was such a test that Dennett and the other philosophers described.

Their suggestions were taken up by the developmentalists Heinz Wimmer and Josef Perner and their colleagues, whose experiments required children to attribute a false belief to another person in the context of a story that was acted out for them with dolls and toys.[7] For example, a boy puts some chocolate in a drawer in the living room and goes out to play. While he's outside his mother moves the chocolate to a cupboard in the kitchen. Then the boy comes back, hungry and wanting his chocolate. He still remembers where he put it. The question is, where will he look for it? Children who correctly predict that the boy will look in the living room drawer recognize the consequences of a person's having a false belief.

Because children have to attribute a *false* belief in order to answer the question, we know they understand that people have beliefs. If the belief they attribute is false, it is necessarily different from their own, whereas if the belief they attribute is true, we would not know whether they were genuinely attributing beliefs to the other person or simply assuming that he or she shared their own beliefs. Or, to put it a different and perhaps better way, they might not be thinking about beliefs at all, but simply assuming that the world is the way it is and they and other people all see it the same way.

In its original form, Wimmer and Perner's task was quite hard even for four-year-olds. When the story was simplified, however, and the salient features made extremely clear, four-year-olds did quite well, but three-year-olds did not. Lou Moses and John Flavell tried even harder to help the three-year-olds. They made stories on videotape, and showed the actor looking in the old place, where he thought the object was—not the real location it had been moved to—and they showed the actor's great surprise when he found a different object in the old place. But even then, although the three-year-olds' performance improved, it was still no better than chance.[8]

Perhaps three-year-olds find it hard to follow a narrative, in a story or on videotape. However, their difficulty with false belief is also evident in real situations, where no story line is involved. Perner and his colleagues showed three-year-olds a Smarties box, a British candy box very familiar to all children (the American equivalent is M & Ms). The children were asked what they thought was inside the box, and they all said "Smarties." But then they were shown that they were wrong—the box actually contained a pencil. They had just had the experience of being misled, of having a wrong belief. Would this help them attribute a false belief to another person? The children were asked what a friend, who had not yet seen inside the box, would think was inside it. Even though they had just gone through the experience themselves, a majority of three-year-olds said the friend would think there was a pencil in the box.[9]

Why weren't the children helped by actually experiencing the false belief themselves? Alison Gopnik and I wondered about this, and thought perhaps it was because it is not simply false belief in others that is hard for three-year-olds to understand. Maybe they don't recognize false belief in themselves either. And indeed, that is the case. Three-year-olds do not understand that their beliefs change: when they find out they were wrong, they are quite unable to remember their own earlier false beliefs.[10] For example, consider a three-year-old who, as in Perner's experiment, thought there were Smarties in the box and then found out it had pencils in it; when the pencils are put back in the box again, if you ask her what she thought was in the box when she first saw it, she'll say "pencils" not "Smarties." Even though she may have said "Smarties" when she first saw the box, she cannot remember this, as my conversation with a three-year-old illustrates:

JWA: Look, here's a box.

Child: Smarties!

JWA: Let's look inside.

Child: Okay.

JWA: Let's open it and look inside.

Child: Oh . . . holy moly . . . pencils!

JWA: Now I'm going to put them back and close it up again. (Does so) Now . . . when you first saw the box, before we opened it, what did you think was inside it?

Child: Pencils.

JWA: Nicky (child's friend) hasn't seen inside this box. When Nicky comes in and sees it . . . When Nicky sees the box, what will he think is inside it?

Child: Pencils.[11]

Heinz Wimmer and Michael Hartl showed that even when the experimenter prompts the child by reminding her what she said at the beginning, some children deny it.[12] You may immediately think that they were embarrassed to admit they were wrong, and were lying to the experimenter in order to cover up their embarrassment. However, in an identical situation, where three-year-olds hear a puppet saying he thinks there are Smarties in the box and then see him find out it's pencils, they also say he thought there were pencils in the box at the beginning.[13] Why? There is no reason to be embarrassed by someone else's mistake and to lie for his sake.

Furthermore, this lying explanation would require that three-year-olds be more embarrassed and more likely to lie than four- and five-year-olds, who are actually quite willing to acknowledge their earlier mistaken beliefs in these experiments. In our experiment children saw five different sets of materials, like the candy box containing pencils, that looked like one thing but turned out to be something else. One five-year-old got the first four tasks right—he was mistaken and then he correctly remembered his own earlier false belief. By the time he got to the fifth task and we showed him a doll (that is actually two dolls), he said suspiciously, "I bet it turns out to be a rabbit!"[14] Such protective skepticism was not available to the younger children. Indeed, understanding false belief and remembering their own false beliefs may help children recognize that things are not always what they appear to be. This is an important realization, which enables them to distinguish between what an object looks like and what it really is in cases where the two do not coincide.

Distinguishing Appearance and Reality

John Flavell and his colleagues have made an extensive study of children's understanding of this distinction between appearance and reality.[15] Their studies began with a visit to the joke store to find objects that appeared to be one thing but were really another, such as a "sponge rock," which is a piece of sponge cunningly painted to look like a lump of granite. Children first saw it from a distance and presumably thought it was a rock. Then they felt it and found out it was a sponge. The "rock" was put back on the table again and the children were asked two questions, "What does this look like?" and "What is it really?" Four-year-olds could answer both of these questions but three-year-olds could not. Once they had found out that it was really a sponge, they said it looked like a sponge. That is, they said it looked like what it really was. For other materials three-year-olds made the opposite error and said things really were the way they looked. For example, three-year-olds said that an orange crayon (which looks black through a blue filter) looked black and really was black, but four-year-olds said it looked black but was really orange. In both cases—the sponge rock and the orange crayon behind the filter—the younger children did not distinguish between the phenomenal appearance and the actual reality.

Flavell and his colleagues made numerous ingenious attempts to uncover the three-year-olds' competence, but without success. In one particularly convincing demonstration they placed a white card under the blue filter with the white edge sticking out. Three-year-olds still said it looked blue and really was blue. Moreover, their problem with these tasks was not simply due to difficulty with the terms *looks like* and *really is*. When the experimenter took a piece out of the card while it was under the filter and then showed the child a white piece and a blue one, three-year-olds chose the blue piece as the one the experimenter had just removed.

From all of these experiments we can see that three-year-olds' difficulties are wide-ranging. They do not understand how someone can believe something different from what they know is actually the case (the false belief task). They do not remember that they themselves once believed something different from what they now know to be true. And they do not understand how something can look different from what it really is. In all of this work great care has been taken to make sure that the particular experimental procedures used do not hide children's understanding.[16] And control tasks have been included to show that three-year-olds can respond to the questions. Even so, they genuinely do not understand false belief.

Nevertheless, it seems not only possible but likely that an understanding of false belief does not arise overnight, and that precursors to this understanding can be found in three-year-olds.[17] Careful and clever experimental work shows that this is indeed the case. For example, if children do not know where the chocolate really is, or if it exists in both locations, then three-year-olds can predict that the character will act on the basis of his belief.[18] However, here no conflict is involved. More strikingly, if three-year-olds are told the true location of the chocolate but do not see it with their own eyes, they are able to predict that the character will look where he thinks it is, in the other cupboard.[19] Three-year-olds are also helped if they are asked where the character will *first* look for the chocolate.[20] In the case of their own false beliefs, three-year-olds can be helped to remember that they mistakenly thought the Smarties box had candy in it, not pencils, if they put a picture of the candy into a mailbox before they see the pencils.[21] Then they are reminded of this when they are asked what they thought was in the box at the beginning. All of this work is important, and it is relevant to the issue of how children arrive at their understanding of the mind—an issue I will take up in the final chapter.

It is equally important, however, to remember that four-year-olds understand others' false beliefs, remember their own false beliefs, and distinguish appearance and reality without these contextual supports, findings that have been widely replicated. What is even more important, a child comes to understand all these things at about the same time. Alison Gopnik and I found significant correlations between children's performance on all of these tasks,[22] and others have found this too.[23] Chris Moore and his colleagues also found that performance on these tasks correlates with performance on a test of children's understanding of the words *think* and *know*.[24] Earlier, John Flavell and his colleagues had shown that understanding the distinction between appearance and reality correlates with the understanding that two people may have different views of the same object, what I referred to in the previous chapter as Level 2 perspective-taking ability.[25]

Representational Theory of Mind

How do we account for these findings? Obviously, children get better at lots of things as they get older. In these studies we have been careful to control for age in looking for relations between different tasks, so the synchronies are not explained simply by the fact that children understand more as they get older, although of course maturation must play some role. We might explain the findings by proposing that some fundamental development underlies performance on all these tasks. What might this be? A number of authors have proposed, in slightly different ways, that children acquire a representational theory of mind at about the age of four.[26]

In Chapter 2 I said that children have two things to discover about the mind, and they might begin with only a partial understanding of representation. At two and three years of age they understand that the mind contains unseen mental entities—thoughts—that are different from things in important ways. However, at this stage they have no understanding of mental activity. This more complete understanding is acquired at about four years of age, when children acquire a representational theory of mind. Then they understand that the mind is active, that it construes and interprets situations. Mental entities are not just things that exist in the mind, they are representations produced by the mind. Once children understand this, they understand that people represent the world and take those representations to be truly the way the world is. They can then see that people do not have direct access to reality but construct the world in their mind, and this constructed world is the world in which people act, even when their representation is a *mis*-representation of the way things really are.

Thus, in order to understand false belief, children have to understand mental activity; they have to understand the representational process. We can see what this entails if we go back to Wimmer and Perner's story, in which the boy put his chocolate in the living room drawer and didn't see his mother move it to the kitchen cupboard. Children have to see that in his mind the boy represents a world in which the chocolate, which they saw moved to the cupboard, is still in the drawer. They have to realize that although the boy's belief refers to the chocolate in the cupboard, it represents it as being in the drawer. And they have to understand that even though he really wants to find the chocolate, the world in which he acts is the world *as he represents it*. They have to be able to coordinate the boy's knowledge of the situation (the way he has construed the world) and their own knowledge (the way things really are). They have to see that what is *true* for the boy (the chocolate is in the drawer) is *false* for them. The way in which they can do this is by distinguishing between the representation *of* something, and representing it *as* something.[27] The boy has a *representation of* the world with chocolate in the new place, the cupboard, but it *represents it as* in the drawer.

The same distinction, between a representation *of* something and representing it *as* something, applies to memory of our own false beliefs. The child who was shown the Smarties box has to see herself as representing a situation where there is candy in the box. She has to understand that this past belief was in fact her representation of reality at that time, even though she later found it to be false. To remember her own false belief she then has to coordinate her present knowledge of the world (pencils in the box) with her past belief (candy in the box) and she has to see that what was true for her then is false for her now. That is, her *representation of* the box of pencils *represented it as* containing candy.

In a similar way, to understand the distinction between appearance and reality, the child again has to understand representational activity. She has to coordinate two conflicting representations. In the case of the sponge rock, the information from one modality (sight) gives false information about the object's true identity. The child has a *representation of* an object that is a sponge, but in looking at it she *represents it as* a rock. The true information about its identity comes through another modality (touch). All of these tasks—understanding another person's false belief, remembering your own false belief, and distinguishing between appearance and reality—thus require an understanding of representations *as* representations, an understanding of representational activity. This is what children achieve when they acquire a representational theory of mind.

Do children all over the world develop a representational theory of mind at four years of age? Since the experiments I have described have all been carried out in daycare centers and nursery schools in Europe and North America, an important question is how universal the findings are. As I said in Chapter 2, there is very little cross-cultural research in the development of folk psychologies—of understanding of mind. We simply do not have enough information to know whether these findings apply universally, and what evidence we do have is equivocal. It would seem that Mandarin-speaking Chinese children understand the distinction between appearance and reality at about the same age as Western children do.[28] A different sort of appearance-reality distinction involves the difference between real and apparent emotion, that is, the difference between someone's real feelings and their facial expression.. At four years of age Western children do not understand this distinction but by age six they do.[29] Similarly, Japanese children also come to understand this distinction between the ages of four and six, despite the profound differences in the extent to which emotions are expressed in the two cultures.[30]

The Chinese and Japanese children in these studies live in non-Western societies, but these societies are literate and the children attend school or preschool. However, a study involving unschooled children from a preliterate society also found evidence that they have an understanding of others' minds at the same age as the children in the Western studies. Jeremy Avis and Paul Harris showed that Baka children of the Cameroon develop the ability to predict action based on a person's false belief at about the age of four.[31] Avis and Harris

propose that there is a universal core to our understanding of mind, essentially the belief-desire-action tri-
angle I described in Chapter 5. They suggest that people
everywhere explain and predict someone else's actions
by considering what that person thinks and wants. More
elaborate conceptions, they suggest, may vary between
cultures. This seems a plausible suggestion, even though
the data do not yet exist to support it, or to refute it.
However, it is important to keep in mind societies whose
conceptions, even quite fundamental ones, are very different from Western ones.

For example, to us in Western society, false belief and
appearance-reality are equivalent. If something looks unlike what it really is, to us that is what someone might
think it to be, or what we ourselves thought it was before
we discovered its true identity. However, it is open to
question whether these two things are universally
equivalent. Penny McCormick has conducted studies
among the Quechua of Peru, peasant people in the high
Andes, whose preliterate culture is undergoing change
as it comes into contact with the dominant Spanish culture. Folktales in the Junin Quechua dialect make no
reference to mental life.[32] There is a story, for example,
of a fox who saw the reflection of the moon in the
water—it looked like a cheese, and the greedy fox dived
in the water to get it, and drowned. When this story was
read to Canadian adults and they were asked to retell it,
they almost all reported that the fox saw the moon's
reflection and thought it was a cheese. Looking like a
cheese or thinking it is a cheese—these expressions are
not very different to us. However, the Junin Quechua
language has no simple way of saying "The fox thought
it was a cheese."

In McCormick's studies, four- to eight-year-old
Quechua children were tested by a native speaker,

known to them, about objects such as the "sponge rock."[33] They were asked about appearance and reality (What does this look like? What is it really?), about what someone would think it was, and about what they themselves thought it was when they first saw it. The *think* questions were asked using the verb *say*, a word they knew well ("What will he say it is?" "What did you say it was?"). The remarkable finding was that the children found the appearance-reality questions much easier than the belief questions. It seems that these children were used to thinking about appearances, and appearances discrepant from reality, but were not used to thinking about what people would think (or say), just as their dialect has a well-developed vocabulary for appearance and reality but not for belief. And yet McCormick reports that tricking is a common and much enjoyed practice among the Quechua people and that they have an extensive vocabulary for talking about lies, which suggests that they do have a conception of false belief, even if they don't talk about it in the same way we do.

Lies and Deception

Lying depends upon understanding false belief. Once children understand that people may hold false beliefs, they are in a position to set about purposely creating a false belief in someone else. Can children deceive others before they understand false belief? Yes and no. People may be deceived by something a child says or does, just as they may be deceived by the rocklike appearance of the painted sponge. However, we may be as reluctant to say that the child has deceived someone as we are to say that the sponge rock has done so. The person is deceived, true, but the sponge rock obviously has no understanding of deception and no intention to deceive, nor may the young child. That is, the child may not have been practicing deception. What a child says or does may cause a person to believe something that is not true, but unless the child intends her words or behavior to have that effect we are reluctant to say that she has deceived the other person. This becomes clearer when we talk about lying because there we have a more articulate set of terms to use.

The commonest way of deceiving others in the everyday world is by lying. We say something we know to be untrue, intending that the other person believe it to be true. In other words, we deliberately create a false belief in the other. For us to consider something a real lie, what is said must be false, and the person who says it must know it is false and want the other person who is listening to think it is true. Only when all three of these elements are present would we really say that someone is lying. If what is said is false but the speaker doesn't know it is false, we call it a mistake. If what is said is false and the speaker knows it is false but doesn't intend anyone to believe it to be true, we might call it a joke, or irony, sarcasm, or metaphor—there are many speech acts of this type.

This definition of lying also excludes some of the transparent untruths very young children tell, such as the child, covered in crumbs, who denies taking a cookie. Or even more transparently, the three-year-old quoted by Marie Vasek, who went to her mother and said, "I didn't break the lamp and I won't do it again."[34] Children may do this to avoid rebuke, or to escape punishment, or to get what they want. It is a routine which is used because it works—sometimes.

Children with very little verbal ability can engage in quite elaborate "deception" of this kind.[35] For example, a little girl, just two years old, is bouncing around the room. She sees some chocolate cake on the table, which she would like, but her mother won't give her any. So she says she's tired, which would normally succeed in getting her some cake, except that her mother doesn't believe her:

Child: Bibby on.

Mother: You don't want your bibby on. You're not eating.

Child: Chocolate cake. Chocolate cake.

Mother: You're not having any chocolate cake either.

Child: Why? ·(whines) Tired.

Mother: You tired? Ooh!

Child: Chocolate cake.

Mother: No chance.[36]

The child's aim is to get her mother to do something, to give her a piece of cake. She may have no thought of getting her mother to believe something, that she is tired, she just knows that if she is tired she might be given some cake. This illustrates the distinction between first-order and second-order intentional systems I discussed in Chapter 2. First-order systems don't think about what the other believes, only about what the other will do, and they act in order to affect the other's actions. Second-order systems also want to affect what others do, but they go about it indirectly, by affecting what others believe— remember the four-year-old who got you out of bed by telling you the bathroom was flooded, so that you would make her breakfast. Second-order systems manipulate people by manipulating their beliefs—they are into tricks, lies, and secrets.

According to this analysis, we would not count as lying those things children say that they know habitually result in certain actions, as Josef Perner points out.[37] Unless we can exclude this possibility, the child may not be deliberately trying to induce a false belief in the other person, even though she may be deliberately trying to influence the other person's behavior by trying to elicit the habitual result. Perner writes of his son Jacob, who at three and a half would use the excuse that he was tired in order to get out of doing things he didn't want to do. Often this made perfect sense and achieved the desired result. But Jacob's lack of understanding of his strategy was revealed when he used the same excuse in an attempt to avoid going to bed!

Is this debate about what is and is not to be counted as lying just an academic question, something for psychologists to argue about? Parents and preschool teachers seem to have the same reluctance to call young children's untruths lies, or at least, deliberate lies. Preschool teachers and mothers of young children were asked at what age they thought children were able to tell a deliberate lie.[38] Only a third of them thought three-year-olds could do so, whereas three quarters of them thought that four-year-olds could. Interestingly, this increase between the ages of three and four closely parallels the increase we find in the results of false belief tasks.

Experiments Investigating Understanding of Deception

The same debate arises in this area that we have met before. How much can we learn by observing children and interviewing their mothers and teachers, and what more is added by experimental work? This is a particularly tricky area in which to conduct experiments. We can tell children stories in which characters make mistakes, play jokes, tell lies, and so on, and ask the children to make judgments of the story characters' behavior. From this we can discover what children think about lies, and how they understand the term *lie*. But it is more difficult to carry out studies in which we ask the children themselves to lie or deceive, although this can be done.

Again, it was Piaget who first investigated children's understanding of lying.[39] He told children pairs of stories in each of which a character said something untrue. For example, a boy who was frightened by a dog went home and told his mother he saw a dog as big as a cow. A second boy told his mother he'd got good marks at school one day, and the mother rewarded him, although that day he'd been given no marks at all. Piaget then asked the child which story character was more naughty. He found that children did not consider intention in making their judgment until age seven or so. Younger children considered how far the statement deviated from the truth, and so an exaggeration caused by fear, as in this example, or an honest mistake as in other stories, received more blame than an intentional misrepresentation of the facts. But notice that the characters' intentions are not made explicit in these stories, they have to be inferred. In addition, Piaget said young children called all factually incorrect statements *lies*, even when the character was simply mistaken.

In a series of carefully controlled experiments, Wimmer, Gruber, and Perner showed that Piaget was half right.[40] Young children do use the word *lie* in the way Piaget said. Until they are six or seven years old children call all untrue statements lies, whatever the intentions of the speaker. However, Wimmer and his colleagues also showed that when speakers' intentions are made clear, children do consider intention in deciding whether to blame those who say things that are untrue. One of the stories the study used was the misplaced chocolate story, described earlier. As in the original false belief task, the children were asked where the boy would look for the chocolate. But then, before he can look for it, his sister appears and asks him where the chocolate is. In one version of the story the children are told that the boy wants his sister to find the chocolate and in another version that he doesn't want her to. (Remember, he thinks it is where it is not!) So in the first version, even though he doesn't intend to deceive her, she doesn't find the chocolate because he has told her to look in the wrong place, where he thinks it is. In the second version, when he does try to deceive her, what he says is actually true because he tells her it is in the place it has been moved to, thinking it is still where he put it. The striking finding is that even four-year-olds did not blame the first boy but they did blame the second one, even though he had actually *said* where the chocolate was. Clearly the children were judging on the basis of intention. However, even so, they still said the first boy—the one who had said something untrue, even though he did not know it was false and did not intend to deceive his sister—had lied and not the second.

Experiments like this are important because they show us that even though children use the same words we use, they may not mean the same things by them. Interestingly, in the interview study I just reported, mothers were asked whether they had explained to their children what a lie was.[41] Most of them said they had, and most of them had told the child it was something that was not true! Only one mother had included in her explanation the fact that the person who said it knew it was not true. Even adults are not entirely in agreement on what they would call a lie, but they consider thinking that what is said is untrue and intending to deceive more important than the actual truth of the statement.[42]

Mistakes and lies are distinguished on the basis of the speaker's beliefs. The difference between the two speech acts depends on the speaker's beliefs about the world. A person who makes a mistake does believe what he himself says, whereas if he tells a lie he doesn't. Sometimes, of course, the person doesn't believe that what he says is true, but he is not telling a lie. He intends it as a joke, or as sarcasm or irony. He doesn't believe that what he says is literally true, and in these cases, he doesn't want the listener to believe it is true either. That is, the difference between a lie and joke depends on the speaker's intentions regarding the listener's beliefs about the world. When do children understand this?

Sue Leekam told children pairs of stories in which she made the contrast between these two cases obvious.[43] For example, in one pair of stories a boy points to a painting on the wall at school and says to his mother, "I did that picture." In one version, the boy then immediately points out the girl's name at the bottom of the picture. He doesn't want his mother to believe he did it, or to go on believing that—it was just a joke. In the other version, the boy says nothing, but the next day when he isn't there his mother sees the girl's name at the bottom of the picture. In both cases the mother eventually knows the boy didn't do the painting. Leekam then asked the children which boy *wanted* his mother to know. She showed that even four-year-olds are able to make this distinction and correctly call one a lie and one a joke. However, it is not until the school years that children distinguish all the different ways in which people don't say what they mean or mean what they say, such as when they use irony to mock someone, tell a white lie to protect someone's feelings, use metaphor to create poetic images, and so on.[44] Children still have a lot to learn after the age of five.

So far, I have discussed only studies that assessed

children's understanding of deception and their comprehension of the relevant linguistic terms. But there is also the question of children's ability to practice deception, which is potentially more difficult to investigate because the experimenter is asking the child to do something that usually meets with adult disapproval—except, that is, in games. Deception may be permitted within the boundaries of a game. In other words, tricking and joking are okay but lying and cheating are not. These are subtle distinctions that we ask children to make.

Michael Chandler and his colleagues have argued that children may find it easier to practice deception than to respond correctly in false belief tasks.[45] Deceptive games are more involving and motivating, they say, and there is no complicated story sequence to follow. By and large, however, we find that children are not able to deceive in these gamelike situations until about the same age as they can pass false belief tasks, that is, at around four years.

It is important, in experiments, to control the situation so that the claims we make are justified. In deception experiments it is important to show that children are not just doing things that *happen* to deceive somebody. We want to know whether they are deliberately acting in such a way as to create a false belief in the other. For this reason, the games are set up so that the child has to deceive one person (or puppet) and help or respond truthfully to another one. The question is, Can the child operate flexibly and understand enough about the beliefs of others to be able both to compete and to cooperate?

Beate Sodian asked children to try to keep a robber puppet from getting a coin and to help a king puppet to find it.[46] The child's motivation was that the robber would take the coin for himself but the king would add another one from his treasure bag and the child could have them both. A coin was hidden in one of two toy trunks before the puppet appeared on the scene, so the child knew where the coin was but the puppet didn't. The puppet then asked the child where it was. The test was to see if the child could prevent the robber from getting the coin by telling him or pointing to the empty trunk, and help the king find it by telling or showing him where it was. Four-year-olds were well able to do this, but three-year-olds were not. They always indicated where the coin was, for both the robber and the king.

But do we know that the three-year-olds understood the task and were interested in keeping the coin for themselves? Yes, we do, because in a second condition, the child had to do something to change the physical situation in order to stop the robber from taking the coin and help the king find it. This time, the robber and the king were lazy, and each of them would open only one trunk. The child's task was to lock one of the trunks so that the robber wouldn't get the coin and the king would. That is, here the child was altering the others' behavior by controlling the physical situation, not altering their beliefs by controlling the information. This was a diffi-cult and perhaps counterintuitive task, because to help the king one has to lock an empty trunk. Even so, the three-year-olds were more successful at this task than when they had to act deceptively and say something untrue or point to the empty location. Because the four-year-olds deceived the robber but not the king, we know they understood that they were affecting the other's be-liefs, but three-year-olds could not do this. However, because the three-year-olds were able to lock the full trunk to defeat the robber and lock the empty one to help the king, we know they understood the task and were motivated to succeed.

Would three-year-olds succeed if they played a game

with a real person rather than a puppet? James Russell and his colleagues set up such a game.[47] A tiny chocolate was hidden in one of two boxes; neither the child nor the other person knew which box it was in. The child had to point to one of the boxes. If it contained the chocolate, the other person won it, but if the chocolate was in the other box, the child did. This was repeated fifteen times to ensure that the child really understood the procedure. Then two boxes with windows that faced toward the child and away from the competitor were substituted for the original boxes. The game was the same. A chocolate was put in one box and the child had to point to a box that the competitor then opened—if the chocolate was there, he got it and if it was in the other box, the child got it. But now the child's task was easy, since she could see where the chocolate was, point to the empty box, and always win. Strikingly, three-year-olds usually pointed to the box containing the chocolate, whereas four-year-olds pointed to the empty box. Over twenty trials, the three-year-olds continued to point to the chocolate, even though they lost it every time. Those four-year-olds who didn't point to the empty box at first soon learned to do so. Russell and his colleagues showed that children's performance on the "windows" task correlated with their performance on a false belief task.

This correlation does not support Chandler's suggestion that deception would be easier than false belief because it is a more realistic and more motivating situation. However, Chandler might argue that Sodian's and Russell's "games" were still rather contrived experimental situations.

It is harder to make this argument for a task that Joan Peskin devised.[48] Her task essentially mimics a situation children experience in real life: someone else wants what they themselves want. As Peskin notes, older siblings soon acquire the strategy of pretending to want another toy when their younger sibling wants the toy they are playing with. Then the younger sibling will switch her preference, and the older sibling can go back to the toy he was originally playing with. In Peskin's task the child played opposite two puppets. She was told that one of the puppets always wanted what the child wanted and would take it if he knew what she wanted, whereas the other puppet would never do that. There were three stickers, one more desirable than the others. The child could choose a sticker for herself, but the puppets got to choose first. Before making his choice, each puppet asked the child which sticker she wanted. Over four trials three-year-olds never learned to tell the selfish puppet that they wanted a sticker other than the desirable one, but four-year-olds quickly learned to do so, if they hadn't done it on the first trial. However, on a trial where there were only two stickers and so only one puppet could play, the three-year-olds understood the situation well enough to exclude the selfish puppet from the game.

This study shows that four-year-old children can be deceptive about their desires or intentions. It reminds me of a family I once knew, with a five-year-old sister and a three-year-old brother. Whenever the children had ice cream cones the sister always said to her brother, "Let's have a race and see who eats it first." The brother always wolfed his ice cream, and then had to watch while his sister slowly licked hers and gloated that she had ice cream and he didn't! Surprisingly, he always fell for the same trick—until he turned four, that is.

Four-year-olds can lie and deceive, it seems, but younger children's ability to do so is still open to question. Chandler and his colleagues have shown that children as young as two can act deceptively.[49] In their game some treasure was hidden in a container by a doll who left inky footprints wherever she went, so a track led to the treasure's location. The child's task was to make it hard for a person who was out of the room while the doll was hiding it to find the treasure when he returned. A majority of children at all ages wiped up the track that led to the treasure and used the doll to lay tracks to empty containers, although some of them needed prompting from the experimenter to do these things. It was unclear whether the children understood the effects of their actions since there was no control condition. A subsequent experiment included a control in which they had to help someone find the treasure.[50] The children, the youngest now just under three, did succeed, but attempts by other researchers to replicate this finding have not succeeded, and so the debate continues.[51]

Whatever the outcome of this debate it seems clear that by age four or five children do understand false belief and can deliberately deceive people.[52] In talking to children about lying, it is more important to emphasize truthfulness than truth. We should always try to tell the truth, to say what we think, but sometimes what we think will not be true and so we will say things that are not true. This isn't telling a lie, it is making a mistake. Telling a lie is when you know what you say is false, you are not being truthful. In emphasizing truthfulness rather than truth, we emphasize the importance of understanding one another's mental states, which is, after all, what is most important in our interpersonal relations—not what we *say* but what we *mean*. Indeed, understanding this distinction between truthfulness and truth may depend in a general way on understanding the distinction between pragmatics and semantics, between what a person means and what his or her statement means. You want the listener to believe what you say because *you* believe it, you think what you say is true—that is, you are being truthful and you can be trusted. Truthfulness and trust are crucial concepts which continue to develop through the school years.[53]

The data I have reported in this chapter can be summarized very briefly: Children come to understand false belief in themselves and in other people at about the age of four. At the same age they start to tell deliberate lies and are able to deceive other people by creating false beliefs in the other. It is perhaps ironic that the result of the child's discovery of the mind is the ability to tell lies and deceive. But this is only one aspect of understanding other people's minds. It also allows us to think about things from others' points of view, to be empathic, to think of what might help or please them. There are some children who seem never to reach this understanding. It is to them that I now turn.

9 / The Undiscovered Mind

What would children's lives be like, what would the children be like, if they never discovered the mind in the way I have described in the previous chapters? This is not an entirely hypothetical question. It is a great tragedy that there are a small number of children who seem not to discover the mind in the normal way in their early years. Such children are autistic.

A Child with Autism

One mother has written a sensitive and moving account of her autistic child's life.[1] Elly was a beautiful blue-eyed, golden-haired baby, the fourth child in an academic New England family. In her early months she was alert and smiling, just as her brother and sisters had been, though of course each child is different and develops differently, as parents of four easily recognize. Elly was slower than the others, slower to walk, slower to talk, but parents of four find it easy not to worry about individual differences. Elly was a placid baby who seemed happy with her own company, unconcerned by the busy family life going on around her. Sometimes she would just sit, for long periods of time, playing with a chain, coiling and uncoiling it. Perhaps she was too self-contained, too self-sufficient for a baby, but that hardly seemed a drawback to a busy mother—perhaps it was an early sign of great inner resources, of future independence. And Elly did progress. By nine months she could sit alone, and at twelve months she crawled. But after her first birthday her progress seemed to slow down, or maybe one expects more as time goes by.

It is sometimes difficult, once a misfortune has arisen, to look back in one's life and try to detect its onset. Were there any signs, warnings, omens? How can one tell, looking back, in knowledge, to the time before one knew? Clara, her mother, wrote, "It is hard to remember the first stirrings of doubt about a baby, but I remember a day when I took Elly to the supermarket. She was nineteen months old. She sat in the shopping cart, alert and intent, her eyes taking in the objects on the shelves as she rolled along."[2] They met a friend with a baby Elly's age who had had a difficult birth, though now she was fine. As Clara watched her, the child looked at her mother and then pointed to a box of candy. Clara realized, at that moment, that she had never seen Elly point. Elly's self-containment was so great that she never showed things, never asked for things, never pointed. She was content with what she was given. Occasionally she would cry violently, but one had to guess what was wrong, she could not say. It might be something seemingly trivial, like her milk not being in its usual container. One had to guess and correct it in order to quiet and comfort her.

What then were the "first stirrings of doubt" and when did they occur? In Elly's first year her parents noticed nothing, nor did her doctor, who saw her for checkups. At thirteen months he deferred a routine vaccination because of eczema, and Elly was twenty-two months old before Clara took her back for it, with the sang-froid of a mother of four. Clara writes, "I was expecting nothing eventful when I carried Elly into the office and set her on the examination table . . . Hard to believe as that seems now, we went to get her vaccinated, not to ask about her strangeness."[3] The doctor was worried, however, and wanted Elly to be tested at the hospital. She wasn't walking or talking—perhaps there were metabolic deficiencies that would explain her slowness. But nothing was found. Elly, although slow, was within normal limits. The pediatrician advised the parents to wait another six months before trying to do anything more. He did not know the family and said Elly seemed like a child who had been raised very much alone. As Clara said, "The diagnosis is already implicit in that sentence. But neither we nor the doctors know that."[4]

Clara did wait, as told, but not passively. She worried about mental retardation. This would perhaps explain the slowness in walking. But Elly's movements, as she bounced in her crib, as she crawled, as she coiled her chain, were so well-coordinated, so delicate, it was hard to think that she was mentally retarded. And there were signs of hidden intelligence. Clara scribbled to encourage Elly to scribble. Clara drew circles and crosses. Elly didn't copy then, in the shared social encounter, but three days later she privately drew a cross, surely a greater feat of intelligence than immediate imitation?

Clara worried that Elly might be deaf, which would explain the slowness in talking. Elly was so self-absorbed, indeed she seemed not to hear anything going on around her—voices, noises—she even ignored a fire engine. But she must have been able to hear because she sometimes turned when someone quietly whistled, she didn't like the dishwasher being turned on, she responded to music, and she knew a few words. If she were deaf she wouldn't know any words. Her word learning was odd, however—words came and then they went. She would use a word for a while but then it disappeared. At two she could speak six words but seemed to understand only two of them. By four years she had used thirty-one words but less than half of these were still in use. And "use" is perhaps not the right word here—"Elly spoke words though not often. But she did not use them to communicate. She had no idea of language as a tool that could cause things to happen."[5] When she wanted something, she didn't ask, she didn't reach or point to it, she picked up someone's hand or arm and threw it toward the thing she wanted, or if what she wanted was further away she would push or lead someone toward it. Elly used the other person as a tool rather than as a helpmate. She didn't use language for communication, indeed, she didn't really communicate.

Clara worried about all these things as she waited. She worried, too, about how she could help Elly, most of all how she could break through Elly's self-containment and make human contact with her. Clara did more than worry, however, she worked with Elly, endlessly and patiently. She played with Elly and tried to get Elly to play. Normal three-year-olds are busy playing all the time, and as they play they learn. They imitate what they have seen others do, often in elaborate pretend games as we saw in Chapter 4. Once Clara saw Elly feed some cereal to a doll, *just once.* Much of her time she was happy not to play, and when she did play, her games were repetitive routines. She had a hundred blocks that Clara used to teach her to build a tower. She did build a tower, though left to herself what she liked to do was arrange the blocks in parallel rows over and over again. She liked shapes, she had some colored parquet shapes. Soon after she was two and a half, she could discriminate diamonds, squares, and triangles, and she could discriminate the different colors too. She liked these abstract, meaningless shapes. Around three years of age she started to do jigsaw puzzles. Again, she could make amazing discriminations of shape and color, but the picture itself was not of much interest or importance to her. She found it just as easy to do a puzzle with the blank side up, the picture face down on the table.

Then Clara's waiting was over. When Elly was about three years old her parents took her to a famous pediatrician in Boston. Clara said that she feared the worst which, for her, was to be told that Elly was mentally retarded. But the doctor did not tell the parents that. He told them, with kindness and hesitation, that the diagnosis was not straightforward but that he thought Elly was autistic.

Autism

Autism is a very rare disorder that was identified and described only fifty years ago. Two psychiatrists, Leo Kanner and Hans Asperger, independently described the syndrome in the early 1940s. The striking characteristic of the children they wrote about was their lack of normal contact with people, their complete self-absorption and emotional solitude, which gave rise to the name "autism" from *autos*, the Greek word for self. Kanner wrote, "these children have come into the world with innate inability to form the usual biologically provided affective contact with people."[6] Whatever else characterizes people with autism, it is their inability to relate to others in an ordinary human way that is most striking, just as we saw in Clara's description of Elly.

Perhaps four in ten thousand children suffer from autism. The precise number depends on the criteria used for diagnosis. However, it is a rare disorder in comparison, for example, to mental retardation, which affects four in one thousand children.[7] More boys than girls are diagnosed as autistic, in a ratio of about four to one. This suggests that it is a disorder of biological origin. It is diagnosed, however, on the basis of behavioral abnormalities. The symptoms used as a basis for diagnosis are very much as Kanner described them, and as Clara observed in Elly's early years.

There are four crucial symptoms. First, there is the abnormality in autistic children's relationships with other people, which leads to their aloneness even in situations where they are surrounded by others. Second, there is impairment in their language development and perhaps more fundamentally, in their ability to communicate even without language—their ability to "get in touch" or "get it across," which I discussed in Chapter 3. In other words, their pragmatic skill, their ability to communicate in an ordinary way, is seriously affected. Third, autistic children do not spontaneously engage in pretend play in the sorts of ways I described in Chapter 4. Autistic children may play with toys in a very repetitive or obsessive way, such as passing a toy from hand to hand repeatedly, as Elly did with her chain, or lining toys up systematically, as Elly did with her blocks. This illustrates the fourth symptom—autistic children's obsession with stereotyped movements or routines or interests.

These are symptoms that do not, indeed by their very nature cannot show themselves at the beginning of a child's life. Thus, as with Elly, there is usually no suspicion of autism during the child's first year. At the present time there is no method for the early diagnosis of autism. Some babies are not socially responsive but become so later on, and some children who are later diagnosed as autistic are quite normal as babies.[8] As one mother wrote, "It is, to my mind, one of the most exquisitely cruel aspects of early childhood autism that it only becomes apparent to the parents very slowly that there is anything wrong with the child."[9] This does not imply that autism is not a genetic defect, simply that it is not evident at the beginning. This is what we would expect if autism is due to a defect in a system that does not mature until the end of infancy. What may be more obvious in infancy is the general mental handicap that is frequently associated with autism. Autistic children often have some degree of mental retardation. However, there are also children with normal or high levels of intelligence who display the characteristic symptoms of autism, as Elly did. These children perhaps display autism in its purest form insofar as whatever damage they have suffered has affected only the critical system underlying social contact and communication, without the widespread damage that leads to mental retardation.[10]

It is still unclear what this critical system is, and thus what causes autism. Soon after the syndrome was first described it was suggested that it might be due to abnormal interactions within the family. This was based on the fact that more middle-class children were diagnosed as autistic, which is no longer the case and might have been due to more referrals from middle-class homes. It was also based on the fact that autism did not seem to run in families. However, this would be unlikely in any case, because autistic individuals very rarely have children of their own and because the disorder itself is so rare. A striking finding in favor of genetic causation is the fact that 2 percent of the siblings of autistic children are autistic. Although this is a very low figure, it is fifty times higher than would be expected by chance. Even stronger evidence is the finding that of eleven autistic children with an identical twin, four of the twin siblings were autistic, whereas of ten autistic children with a fraternal twin, none of the twin siblings was autistic.[11] Thus the idea that was prevalent in the fifties—that the mother's coolness and inability to relate to her child caused the disorder—has been quite thoroughly overturned.

It seems clear that the disorder is biological in origin, although precisely what is wrong is still unclear. The search is for an underlying deficit that would explain all the symptoms of autism—the abnormalities in social relations, in language development, and in play. As we have seen throughout this book, children's acquisition of folk psychological understanding, their discovery of the mind, underlies their interpersonal relations and ordinary language use. Perhaps, somehow, autistic children fail to discover the mind.

Does the Autistic Child Have a Theory of Mind?

Simon Baron-Cohen was one of the many people who read Premack and Woodruff's paper "Does the Chimpanzee Have a Theory of Mind?" (see Chapters 1 and 8). He was struck by Dennett's comments, particularly his description of young children's gleeful delight as they watch Punch and Judy. Baron-Cohen realized that autistic children would not react in such a way. Perhaps, he thought, these children do not develop a theory of mind as normal children do. In collaboration with Uta Frith and Alan Leslie he designed a task to try to answer this question.[12] Children were asked to arrange four pictures into a sequence and to tell the story. There were three types of sequences. The first type, mechanical stories, depended on physical interactions between objects and people—for example, a man kicks a rock so that it rolls down a hill and splashes into the water. The second type depended on behavioral interactions between people—for example, a girl takes a boy's ice cream cone and eats it herself. The third type of story was best described at a mentalistic level—for example, a girl puts her toy down behind her while she picks a flower, someone takes it away, and the girl turns around and is surprised to find it gone. Baron-Cohen and his collaborators compared the ability of autistic children aged six to seventeen to do this task with that of Down Syndrome children of a similar age range and normal four-year-olds. The average verbal and nonverbal mental age of the autistic children was higher than that of the other two groups. Despite this advantage, the autistic children performed worse than either of these groups on the mentalistic stories, although they were as good or better than the other two groups on the mechanical and behavioral stories. In the mentalistic stories the autistic children could not attribute, for example, the mental state of surprise to a character and use it to make sense of the sequence.

At about this time, Wimmer and Perner's paper describing the false belief task was published.[13] Baron-Cohen, Leslie, and Frith devised a simple version of this task for the autistic children, again comparing their performance with that of the Down Syndrome children and normal four-year-olds.[14] They found that most of the four-year-olds and the Down's children, but very few of the autistic children, were able to predict correctly that a doll character who did not see her marble moved from a basket to a box would look for it in the original location, in the basket. That is, the autistic children could not attribute a false belief to the doll.

These two studies provided early and compelling evidence that autistic children do not develop a theory of mind as normal children do, which would explain both their social and pragmatic difficulties. If autistic children are unaware of the mind, if they are unable to attribute mental states to others, it is not surprising that they relate to other people as objects and that they are socially isolated. Similarly, if they cannot take account of people's beliefs and intentions, ordinary communication becomes impossible.

Subsequent investigations confirmed and extended these findings. Perhaps it occurred to you that the autistic children might have had difficulty with the doll scenario because they do not engage in pretend play. Perhaps so. However, they are also unable to attribute false beliefs to others in cases where the scenario is acted out with real people and they are part of the interaction.[15] And they find the "unexpected contents" false belief task just as difficult. Once they themselves have found out that an ordinary looking candy box has a pencil in it, they can't understand that someone else, who just sees the outside of the box, will think it has candy in it.[16] Nor can autistic children create false beliefs by deceiving others, for example, in the kind of experiments that I described in Chapter 8—they can't tell a lie in order to keep the robber from getting the coin[17]—nor can they point to what they know is an empty box so that the other person doesn't win the chocolate.[18] Autistic children are also unable to distinguish between appearance and reality. Once they have discovered that what looks like an egg is really a stone, they say it both looks like and really is an egg (or looks like and really is a stone). That is, they are unaware of their own mental states; they cannot distinguish between their perception of the object and their knowledge about it.[19] They are also unaware of their own earlier false beliefs. They do not remember that their own belief changed when they found out they were mistaken.[20] Indeed, David Olson has remarked on the irony of the label "autism" from the Greek for *self*, since it seems that autistic people have little self-awareness.

Autistic children's differences from other children are

seen not only in these experimental tasks but also in natural observations. Helen Tager-Flusberg analyzed spontaneous speech samples from six autistic children and six Down Syndrome children of similar age and language ability. She found that the autistic children were like the Down Syndrome children in the way they talked about desire and emotion, but they were less likely than the Down's children to refer to cognitive mental states using words such as *think* and *know.* They talked about perception as the Down Syndrome children did, but they were much less likely to call their mothers' attention to things with words such as *look* and *see.*[21]

Like three-year-olds, autistic children do not attribute false beliefs to others, cannot deceive others, do not remember their own false beliefs, and cannot distinguish between appearance and reality. However, they are not like three-year-olds in other ways, in the sort of ways I described in Chapter 4, for example. Autistic children do not pretend, and they find pretense and imagination difficult to understand in experimental tasks.[22] They do not understand the distinction between thoughts and things, between real and mental entities, as normal three-year-olds do.[23] As Tager-Flusberg showed, they do talk about desires, and do have some understanding of desire, but unlike normal three-year-olds they find it hard to understand that people are unhappy when their desires are not fulfilled.[24]

Thus, autistic children are not simply delayed in their development. They are quite different from other children in these specific ways: in their lack of awareness of the mind, and of their own and others' mental states. The autistic children in the experiments I have just described come from the top third of the autistic population, since they need to have levels of intelligence and language skill sufficient for them to be tested. Their mental age on verbal tests is at least four years, their non-verbal mental age is higher, and their real ages range from six to eighteen and average about twelve years. Their performance is compared with normal four-year-olds and language-delayed children with similar or lower verbal mental age. The general finding is that most of the children in these comparison groups pass the tasks and most of the autistic children fail, despite the advantage of their higher mental age. The autistic children pass control tasks that do not require the attribution of mental states.

All of this helps us to see how profound and specific the autistic child's deficit is, but it gets us no closer to answering the question of what, precisely, is wrong. Or rather, it leads to a bigger question. We say that autistic children's difficulties occur because they do not discover the mind, they do not develop a theory of mind. The bigger question is, How do normal children discover the mind? What *causes* the development of folk psychological understanding in normal children? These questions have been touched on throughout the book, and I will address them specifically in the final chapter. Here I will look at contributions from the study of autism by looking at how the question "What causes autism?" has been answered.

What Causes Autism?

As I said earlier in the chapter, there is no clear answer to this question. Autism is believed to be a biological disorder, a deficit in some innate mechanism. There is argument whether this is fundamentally an emotional deficit or fundamentally a cognitive one.

Kanner himself, in first describing the syndrome, proposed that it was fundamentally an emotional disorder. He said, as I quoted him earlier, that the children he described were *innately unable* to make the sort of affective, that is emotional, contact with other people that usually happens naturally. Autistic children are not unfeeling, and they express their emotions, laughing and crying for example, although some of their facial expressions are unusual and hard to interpret.[25] They talk about emotion, as Tager-Flusberg showed, and they have some understanding of how situations and desires lead to emotions.[26] They can also recognize other people's emotions, at least they see the smiles and frowns, but in experimental tasks they are unable to match a smiling face to a happy voice or a joyful gesture or a picture of a situation that would make someone feel pleased.[27] They somehow don't appreciate the deeper meaning of emotions. They don't understand the significance of other people's emotions. Most strikingly, they don't show empathy toward others.

According to Peter Hobson, these findings support the view that autism is fundamentally an emotional disorder.[28] As I said in Chapter 2, emotions are not hidden in the way that beliefs and desires are. They are expressed naturally and can be perceived by others. Hobson argues that, right from birth, we have a biologically based capacity to perceive others' emotions. This is what autistic children lack, and hence their difficulties begin very early in life. As infants, they do not see the feelings behind others' bodily expressions, nor do they experience emotional communication, that is, psychological connectedness, with their caregivers. It is here, Hobson says, that the child's discovery of the mind begins. Autistic children miss this starting point. Without this foundation stone they have no insight into the mental life of others or of themselves.

This may indeed be the way, or at least part of the way, in which children discover the mind, as we saw in Chapter 3. However, this may not be where autistic children's development goes awry. Their difficulties may arise later. If we were to accept that autism is primarily an emotional disorder with this very early origin, we would be left with two puzzles: first, why some children who are later diagnosed as autistic have apparently normal social relationships in infancy, and second, why autistic children have the particular pattern of deficits that they do.

As I said earlier in this chapter, some babies who are later diagnosed as autistic are quite normally socially responsive as infants, as Elly was, and develop normal attachments to their mothers.[29] Furthermore, a longitudinal study suggests that autistic children's social difficulties do not begin in infancy. In a large sample of one- to three-year-old children who were referred to a clinic because their development was not quite normal, fifty were identified as "not relating to people as persons"— the deficit in interpersonal relatedness that is so characteristic of autism. When the children were followed up some years later, all were found to be mentally retarded to some degree. However, none of the children whose interpersonal deficit had been identified before their first birthday was autistic, but about a quarter of those so identified in their second year, and more than four-fifths of those identified after their second birthday were. This is hard to explain if, as Hobson suggests, autistic children's problems arise from their initial inability to establish interpersonal relations.

Second, if autism is fundamentally an emotional deficit leading to an inability to relate to others, it is hard to explain the particular pattern of autistic children's symptoms. Their difficulty, although profound, is quite specific. They do not find all social cognitive tasks problematic, only those that require the attribution of *mental* states. They perform well on tests of social cognition that do not require the awareness of others' minds.[30] For example, they can recognize themselves in the mirror, identify peers in photographs, distinguish between animates and inanimates, and recognize characteristics of people, such as age, gender, and relationships like mother-child and husband-wife. In perceptual role-taking tasks they can judge what another person sees, although they cannot judge what the other person knows on the basis of what he or she has seen.[31]

These puzzles lead to the suggestion that autism may be caused by a primarily *cognitive* deficit which has secondary emotional consequences. Alan Leslie has suggested that this is a *metarepresentational* deficit. As we saw in Chapter 4, Leslie proposes that an innate brain mechanism, the Theory of Mind module, underlies the cognitive ability to metarepresent. Recall that primary representations are beliefs about the world. Secondary representations, or metarepresentations as Leslie calls them, are suspended from the world, embedded in relationships such as *think* and *pretend*. They take the form, "Sally *thinks* her marble is in the basket," "I *pretend* the banana is a telephone," and so on. Leslie proposes that the mechanism that produces these metarepresentations is impaired in autism.[32] This would explain why autistic children cannot attribute mental states and why they do not engage in pretend play. It would also explain why autistic children do not have difficulty with social tasks that require only primary representation.

Uta Frith supports Leslie's analysis and situates it within her own wider theory, which takes into account the additional characteristics of autistic children, beyond their social isolation, pragmatic difficulties, and lack of pretend play. This is set out in her recent book *Autism: Explaining the Enigma*,[33] which I highly recommend as an interesting, informative, and lucid account of autism. Frith argues that autistic children's fundamental cognitive problem is a deficit in central information processing, specifically an inability to integrate separate pieces of information into meaningful wholes. Recall Elly's jigsaw puzzles—she was just as well able to do the puzzle if the picture was face down on the table. She focused on the shape of individual pieces rather than being guided by the whole picture.

Normally, Frith says, the brain exhibits a strong central drive for cohesion, for overall sense and structure. This is why we find it easier to remember the gist of something than to recall it verbatim, which is not the case for autistic people. And it is why we find it hard to pick out a hidden figure when it is disguised by being part of a larger picture, whereas autistic children are very good at that task because of their weak drive for cohesion. Frith also explains autistic children's social and communicative problems as arising from this same source. When we interact with people we don't focus on individual actions; rather, we integrate information about the person, the event, and the behavior, interpret it in the light of our expectations and presuppositions, and respond to its overall meaning. Autistic children cannot do this because they lack this central drive for cohesion. Their social interaction thus appears detached and uninvolved. Similarly, in conversation, communication depends on a high-level drive for overall sense. We don't respond to what is literally said but to what the person means, taking into account the context, our expectations based on who they are, our presuppositions from what has already been said, and so on. Autistic people, on the other hand, give a literal interpretation to individual statements. In their conversation one thing doesn't lead to another. There is no flow, for example, in Frith's conversation with Ruth, an able, autistic seventeen-year-old:

UF: . . . you live in that lovely flat upstairs?

R: Yes-suh. [Ruth always emphasizes the final consonant]

UF: Is that really good?

R: It is.

UF: Do you do some cooking there?

R: Yes, I do.

UF: What kinds of things do you cook?

R: Anything.

UF: Really. What is your favourite food?

R: Fish fingers.[34]

It was, as Frith says, a very limited communication. Each question and answer was a separate small unit, with no drive for continuity. Frith thus draws together the various difficulties autistic people have. In her theorizing, she is driving for overall sense and structure, and supposes that autistic children's failure to discover minds in behavior is part of this larger picture of autism.

Simon Baron-Cohen also endorses Leslie's position, with an important addition. He is interested in finding the earliest evidence of metarepresentational ability in normal children, before pretend play begins, and determining whether this too is disrupted in autism. He argues that the ability begins around nine months of age, in the first stages of communication and shared attention that I discussed in Chapter 7. Attending is more than looking, it is deliberately looking at an object of interest, that is, it is *about* something. Thus attention is an *intentional*, or representational mental state (see Chapter 2).

Therefore understanding attention is metarepresentational. It is the first metarepresentational ability children acquire, Baron-Cohen argues.[35] As I reported in Chapter 3, normal babies use the direction of their mother's gaze to detect what is the focus of her attention. Autistic children don't do this, nor do they point to direct an adult's attention. Remember Clara's "first stirrings of doubt" when she realized that Elly had never pointed. Autistic children can point if they want to be given something, but they don't point to direct another person's attention, and as I mentioned earlier, they don't call their mother's attention to things using *look* and *see*.

Moreover, since we focus our attention on our goals, that is, we look at things we are trying to do, Baron-Cohen argues that babies who have the metarepresentational ability to understand attention will also use eye direction to detect a person's goal.[36] If an adult holds out a toy to a baby and then teasingly pulls it away as the baby reaches for it, the child looks to the adult's eyes seeking the reason behind the action. Similarly, if the baby is playing with a toy and the adult covers it with her hands, the baby immediately looks to her eyes, again to see why she is doing that. Young autistic children do not react in this way in either of these situations; rather, they look to the adult's hands. They seem to lack an understanding of attention, perhaps because they lack metarepresentational ability.

Currently, Baron-Cohen is conducting a large-scale longitudinal study assessing babies' understanding of attention—their ability to direct someone's attention by pointing, to use eye direction to gauge the focus of someone's attention, and so on. His aim is to find the very earliest indicators of autism.[37] Interestingly, Baron-Cohen's work with autistic children has directed our attention back to the period that Inge Bretherton and her colleagues focused on more than a decade ago when they claimed that a theory of mind was implicit in infants' early attempts at communication.[38] And again, the same questions arise that I considered in Chapter 3, questions concerning the implicit nature of the understanding that is demonstrated in infants' activity and how real that understanding is. Baron-Cohen's work also reminds us of the importance of human communication—that it is an interaction of minds—and that it may be in their attempts to communicate that children first discover the mind.

Individual Differences in Autism

Difficulty with communication is perhaps the most striking feature of autism, although individuals vary in how severe these difficulties are. As I have said, autism is frequently associated with varying degrees of mental retardation, which in itself leads to problems with language and communication. However, even people with autism who have normal levels of intelligence vary in how severe their autistic symptoms are.

Earlier, in describing the experimental tasks, I said that a *majority* of autistic children did not attribute mental states to others or to themselves. However, these experiments also showed that in some individuals there is some development of the ability to attribute mental states, although only after a severe delay. Generally, about a fifth or a quarter of autistic children tested can pass false belief tasks, but at a mental age well beyond four years. These tasks test understanding of people's beliefs about the world, as in "Sally thinks her marble is in the basket." Almost all of these children fail a more difficult task normal six-year-olds pass, which assesses their understanding of one person's belief, about another person's belief as in "Anne thinks that Sally thinks her marble is in the basket."[39] A very few autistic individuals do pass this more complex task. However, even their communicative abilities are not completely normal. They have difficulty with the subtleties of conversation, with jokes and puns, with euphemism.

In an interesting series of studies Francesca Happé has recently demonstrated correlations between communicative competence and these different levels of belief understanding.[40] Autistic people who did not pass any false belief tasks were unable to understand any figurative language unless it was explicitly marked using "like" to indicate a simile, as in "The dog was so wet. It was like a walking puddle." They could not make sense of figurative language without this explicit linguistic marker. They could not understand the metaphor "The dog was so wet. It really was a walking puddle," which can *only* be interpreted nonliterally. Those who passed standard false belief tasks could understand such metaphors. However, unless they also passed the more complex false belief tasks, indicating understanding of people's beliefs about beliefs, they could not comprehend irony, as in, "What a nice dry dog." And even these most able autistic people had some difficulty giving explanations of story characters' nonliteral remarks in more complex, naturalistic stories.[41] Using Sperber and Wilson's Relevance Theory,[42] Happé shows that similes can be understood as descriptions of the world, as primary representations, that metaphors can only be understood by representing the speaker's intention, that is, as metarepresentations, and that irony requires understanding the speakers' intentions about their intention to communicate. She then points out the precise links between the levels of social understanding (in the belief tasks) and levels of communicative understanding (in the language tasks) and demonstrates that in people with autism the same level of impairment is evident in both tasks.

The few very able autistic people who have highly developed language skills and can live relatively normal lives still have difficulty with the more subtle aspects of communication, such as humor, tact, and politeness. Although they may learn to compensate for their disability, in some sense it is in a way that we might in learning a foreign language. The understanding does not come naturally to them. There is no cure for autism, only compensation.

In an epilogue to her book about Elly's early years, Clara, her mother, appends a psychologist's report from intelligence tests Elly was given at the age of about eighteen. He remarked that Elly still had difficulty with the subtleties of social situations, although in some ways she had learned to compensate. "On several Picture Arrangement items she arrived at technically correct solutions even though she did not understand the story or its humor. Her solution was based on sequence and time cues which she picked up quite perceptively."[43] Elly still had difficulty understanding people's thoughts and feelings, but as she grew older she realized that she did and tried to learn about them. At fifteen she had asked, "Is it hurt people's feelings when I cry on the bus?"[44] (her shrill crying was a dreadful noise) and her mother had patiently explained that it hurt people's *ears*, not their *feelings*. The difference between a physical hurt and an emotional hurt was obviously an incomprehensible one to Elly. However, she continued to try to learn, from the outside as it were. New techniques of behavior therapy helped her, and at twenty-one, she began to learn a new category of behavior, "Thinking of Others," and this continued. At twenty-three she was at home with two students while her parents were away on vacation. She had missed them at first, but the students soon discovered that she could be cheered up by the recitation of one of her favorite things, radio station call numbers— "WMNB-FM" they would say, and Elly would smile. One day one of the students heard that her father had been in an accident and was in a coma, and she was dreadfully distressed. "[Elly] could see tears, she did not need to be told that Tracy was sad. She put herself in Tracy's place the best way she knew. She said, not 'I hope you will feel better,' but 'WMNB-FM.'"[45] One smiles with a tear in the eye, and is reminded of the one-year-old who comforts a crying friend with the offer of his own teddy-bear. There is no cure for autism, no complete recovery. Autistic people never really discover the other's mind.

10/Causes and Consequences

I said at the beginning that I had two stories to tell. One was the story of children's discovery of the mind, the other the story of psychologists' investigation of children's discovery of the mind. I cautioned that the children would not describe their discoveries in the terms the psychologists used. This will now be clear. I, of course, have taken the psychologists' viewpoint and used their terms—*belief, desire, representation,* even "discovery of the mind." No five-year-old would talk or think in this way. Indeed, there is a sense in which it is misleading to talk of the child's discovery of the *mind,* of the mind's causing action, and so on. The child—and we ourselves—are less aware of the mind than of the self: it isn't my mind, it's *me.* Similarly, an awareness of others' minds is more an awareness of other selves: it's not his mind, it's *him.* And of course this is the way we talk. We don't say, "My mind held a false belief that the chocolate was in the drawer." Of course not, we say, "*I thought* the chocolate was in the drawer." When I act intentionally, it doesn't seem that my mind causes my action, I do! Similarly, we don't talk of another person's mind holding beliefs, desires, and intentions; rather, we talk of what the person him or herself *thinks, wants,* and so on. We psychologists can talk of children's acquisition of the concepts of belief and desire, but the children themselves will talk of what people think and want. We can talk of their discovery that the mind is active, that it construes and interprets situations, but they do not experience it in such a way or in such terms. The child finds pencils in the candy box. Her experience, that is, her construal of her experience, is not that her mind held a false belief, a belief which referred to a situation in the world but described it differently from the way the world actually was. She feels that she herself was mistaken. She thought one thing and now she knows that something else is actually the case.

In this book I have traced the development of the child's discovery of the mind, sketched in the psychologist's terms. It would be a mistake to create the impression that every child goes to bed the evening before his or her fourth birthday having just failed a false belief task and wakes up next morning ready to pass. Just as there are individual differences in autistic children's achievements, so too with other children. Nonetheless, it is possible to give a general picture of children's development, of their coming to understand their own and others' mental states, and to use this understanding to explain and predict people's behavior. We saw that this discovery begins in infancy with recognition of the distinction between people and things and the intention to communicate with people, not things. It continues in the toddler years when children become able to think of absent and hypothetical things and events—possible alternatives to those really currently present—perhaps best expressed in their pretend play. Here, children are able to distinguish between thoughts and things. Soon, children start to talk about the mind or, at least, about what they and others, see, want, and feel, and then later, think and know too. And young preschoolers have some understanding of perception, desire, and emotion and can use this understanding to predict what people will do. Later they also have some understanding of knowledge and belief. Toward the end of the preschool years children acquire the critical understanding of false belief and recognize that people act in the world as they represent it, even when the representation actually misrepresents the real situation. Individual children arrive at these understandings at slightly different ages, but there is amazing uniformity amid the apparent diversity. Even though there is much more they will learn through the school years and into adulthood, we seem justifed in concluding that by the age of five children have discovered the mind.

I have told the psychologist's story and described the child's development. Two large questions remain, two questions that psychologists who work in this area are currently grappling with. The first concerns causes and the second concerns consequences. First, what causes this development? That is, how does the child discover the mind? Second, what consequence does this development have? That is, how are children's lives changed by their discovery of the mind? These are the issues to which I now turn. They are, as I say, matters of current debate.

How Does the Child Discover the Mind?

Psychologists generally spend more time describing children's development than explaining how that development comes about. As Susan Carey has said, one obvious reason for this is that we cannot begin to explain developmental changes until we know what they are.[1] Another reason, Carey suggests, is that sometimes description *is* explanation. What the toddler, for example, can understand and do, constrains what she learns about the world, and in this sense explains what she learns. Thus, a description of the younger child's ability is an explanation of what enables the development of the older child's ability. Therefore, Carey concludes, descriptive research is necessary and important.

Certainly, the last ten years have seen intensive description of children's folk psychology, which I have summarized in this book. This description provides the data base, the evidence, that requires explanation. It is an oversimplification, of course, to suggest such a neat separation between evidence and explanation. As Carey said, sometimes evidence is explanation. And, as I noted at the beginning, whether we collect data by observation or experiment, we are guided by our theories as to what we will observe or what we will measure in an experiment. Theory determines where we look, and what we find may help redefine the theory. Evidence and explanation are interdependent. Indeed, as I described the data in the earlier chapters I inevitably referred, at least implicitly, to various theoretical explanations. In Chapter 4 I described Alan Leslie's proposal that the brain has a special innate mechanism, a "theory of mind module" that facilitates children's understanding of pretense and other mental states. In Chapter 6 I mentioned Judy Dunn's longitudinal studies and her finding that more family talk about emotions led to children's better understanding of emotion later on. And in Chapter 8 I discussed the idea that children's conceptual development, specifically their acquisition of the concept of representation, underlies their understanding of belief and of people's actions based on false beliefs. These are all theoretical explanations, or hints toward theoretical explanations. Now I will consider them more explicitly.

The phrase I keep using, the very title of the book, *The*

Child's Discovery of the Mind, implies that the mind is there to be discovered. I do not call it the child's *invention* of the mind, as David Olson has done.[2] I do not mean that the mind is there to be discovered in the same way that fingers and toes are. As Bruno Snell has argued, our Western view of humanity began with the Greeks.[3] He traces the origins of our ideas of subjectivity and individual responsibility in Greek literature, beginning before Homer with the pre-Socratic philosophers. These ideas are captured in our folk psychology and are fundamental to our conception of ourselves and others. In this sense "mind" is a cultural invention, and children discover the mind as they acquire the language and social practices of the culture.

In an insightful essay, Carol Feldman explores how our investigation of children's understanding of mind can be situated within the new cultural psychology.[4] For Feldman and for many others, psychology is an interpretive human science, not a causal empirical one. For her, our concern as psychologists, like the child's concern as discoverer of the mind, is not so much to explain and predict people's behavior as to understand and interpret it. What matters is how the child comes to give meanings to what people do, and this is what we must investigate—not with too Piagetian a view of the child as a "little scientist" constructing her own causal theory, but with a more Vygotskian perspective of the child internalizing her culture's construal of mind.

Jerome Bruner has long emphasized the importance of culture in human development.[5] In *Acts of Meaning* he eloquently describes how children learn to make sense of the world, especially the social world, as they acquire the ability to tell stories about it.[6] He shows how children come to use narratives to integrate what they and others think, feel, and do. The important point is that the narrative not only tells what happened but tells it against a background of what usually happens or what ought to have happened, and from a particular point of view. The "same" happening may be recounted quite differently by the child who took the toy and the sister whose toy it is, or by the child who is helping his mother and the mother whose activity is interrupted. Judy Dunn's studies provide many examples.[7] For example, David has just mended three-year-old Megan's toy vacuum cleaner, and now they both want to play with it:

David to mother:	I wanted to do it. Because I fixed it up. And made it work.
Mother to David:	Well, you'll have to wait your turn . . .
Mother to Megan:	Are you going to let David have a turn?
Megan to mother:	I have to do it. *Ladies* do it.
Mother to Megan:	Yes, ladies do it. Yes, and men do it sometimes. Daddy sometimes does the hoovering, doesn't he? . . . so you let David do it.[8]

Thus, in learning to talk, telling and hearing stories in everyday family life, the child learns what can be done and what can't be done, and how people think and feel about it. In other words, she acquires the folk psychology of her culture.

This argument is supported by findings, such as those of Penny McCormick reported in Chapter 8, that in different cultures children respond differently to questions about what someone will say and do, for example, in situations where the person has been misled. Indeed, it could be argued that different cultures talk about these things in such different ways that we cannot compare across cultures.[9] On the other hand, evidence such as that provided by Avis and Harris,[10] that children from very different cultures all have the same basic understanding of how beliefs and desires determine actions and feelings, undermines the view that folk psychology is acquired by enculturation, or at least suggests that there is some basic similarity to all cultures' understanding of these things. However, the evidence from autistic children's development more seriously undermines the Enculturation viewpoint. Elly, whom I wrote about in the previous chapter, grew up in the same social environment as her brothers and sisters but she did not discover the mind in the way they did. As I said then, it is generally agreed that autism is a disorder that is biological, not social in origin. Thus, although it may be true that "mind" is a cultural invention, there is still a sense in which each child discovers the mind for herself. The question is, how?

It was the evidence from autistic children's development that led Leslie to propose that there is an innate component underlying children's discovery of the mind. The nativist viewpoint is also supported by research with close relatives to humans, such as apes, which shows that they too can attribute inner states to other members of their species.[11] However, this only shifts the burden of explanation from developmental psychologists to biologists. If children's understanding is innate, then we would want to know how it arose in the course of evolution.

The suggestion that folk psychological understanding is based on innate mechanisms or structures does not necessarily imply that this understanding is present from birth. Indeed, we have seen that it is not. There is considerable development during the first five years. Nonetheless, babies seemed to be tuned into people right from the start, as I described in Chapter 3, which may indicate innate precursors that facilitate the discovery of the mind. Few would argue this point. Everyone seems to agree that there is an innate initial state that is impaired in autism, but many people argue that these initial structures or capacities are then modified with development. This view does not imply that children in all cultures will develop in the same way. It allows for variation due to different experiences. It allows for conceptual development.

Leslie makes a much stronger argument, however. He says that the brain has a "theory of mind module" and that this is what is impaired in autistic children.[12] His view does allow for development with maturation—the module is triggered in some way in the second year, leading to the beginnings of pretense and later to the understanding of other kinds of mental states, such as beliefs. But the module constrains that development in a precise way. Experience might trigger the module but it cannot modify it. Regardless of experience, children everywhere will develop the same understandings. Understanding is not constructed by the child.

The Enculturation viewpoint emphasizes the role of socialization and the Nativist viewpoint emphasizes the role of biological maturation in explaining children's development. Lying between these two views are theories that consider the child's role in constructing knowledge through conceptual development. Piaget's is such a viewpoint. Piaget's concern, however, was not to explain children's development in a particular domain, such as their folk psychological understanding, but to provide an overall explanation of development based on a few fundamental concepts. I mentioned one of these, *egocentrism*, in the first chapter. Piaget first used this term to characterize aspects of young children's language and later to characterize their thought more generally. Piaget's work on egocentrism inspired a lot of developmental research in the 1960s and 1970s. The focus of this work was on children's *role-taking* ability, that is, their success in overcoming egocentrism, and their ability to take another person's point of view. You "put yourself in the other person's shoes," as it were, and then you know how the world looks to him or her. This ability was thought to underlie much of children's social cognitive development.

More recently, Paul Harris has described a mechanism by which role-taking might operate, what he calls *simulation*.[13] Like Carl Johnson,[14] Harris emphasizes that beliefs and desires are mental states the child actually experiences. In their view, even young children can introspect their own mental states and are intuitively aware of their own phenomenal experience. Harris says that children don't predict people's actions by using laws linking beliefs and desires, but by imagining themselves having the beliefs and desires that the other person has, and imagining what they themselves would do if they possessed those imagined beliefs and desires. He says that this ability, to simulate another person's experience and to simulate their actions and reactions, depends on three abilities that develop in the preschool years.[15]

First, as we've seen, young children have a great capacity for pretense. They start to pretend at about eighteen months of age and over the next year or two, as their pretend play develops, they are able to ascribe pretend mental states to dolls and take on pretend states themselves. For example, they pretend the doll wants a drink or that they want a cookie. Second, young children can reason with pretend premises. For example, if they pretend to want a cookie and someone pretends to give them one, they can pretend to be happy and pretend to eat it. Third, children are able to alter what Harris calls their *default settings*, which form the background against which the child operates. They consist of the child's own current mental states and the current state of the world (as it is known to the child). Role-taking, or simulation of another person's experience, involves alteration of these default settings. It involves, for example, setting aside one's own desires and/or beliefs and taking on those of the other person in order to simulate what the other person will do or how she'll feel. The more default settings that need to be suspended, the more difficult the simulation will be. To understand false belief, for example, the child has to imagine a nonexistent situation that substitutes for a portion of known reality, for example, that a hidden object is in its original location. Then she has to adjust her stance to that substitute bit of reality. She doesn't believe it, but she has to imagine the other person does believe it. This is more difficult than simply imagining someone wanting something different from what the child herself wants, and so is not achieved until a later stage.

The Enculturation viewpoint emphasizes the role of socialization and the Nativist viewpoint that of biological maturation, while the Simulation view emphasizes the role of the child's own introspective experience. According to this view, the child derives an understanding of psychological concepts—concepts of belief, desire, intention, emotion—from her own experience. There is a fourth view that also emphasizes the importance of the child's experience and likewise claims that the child takes an active role in constructing her understanding of mind. This is the view that the child develops a theory of mind.

Is It Really a Theory of Mind?

In the 1960s and 1970s hundreds of articles were published that had "role-taking" in the title, while in the 1980s and currently "role-taking" is out of fashion and there are hundreds with "theory of mind" in the title. One might wonder if this suggests a general change in the way psychologists explain the child's discovery of the mind, a change of allegiance from a simulation viewpoint to a theory view. To a certain extent, this may be true, but not entirely. Josef Perner reports a conversation with John Flavell about Flavell's 1968 monograph, *The Development of Role-taking and Communication Skills in Children*.[16] Perner asked Flavell whether his use of the term "role-taking" implied that he was taking a simulation view in explaining the development of children's abilities, and Flavell said that it did not. He used the term simply because at that time it was the usual label for the development of social cognition. I think this might be quite generally true. Psychologists' main concern has been to describe such development. Their theories about what caused the development would reflect the general theoretical stance they took, whether Piagetian, social learning, information processing, or whatever.

Now the phrase "theory of mind" has taken over from "role-taking" in the developmental literature, and just as Flavell said that his use of "role-taking" in 1968 implied no allegiance to the Simulation view, so today, some people who use the term "theory of mind" are not thereby implying that they believe that the child actually develops a *theory* about the mind. The phrase "theory of mind" is used in at least three different ways. First, it is used simply to designate a research area, as the term role-taking was. It is even used in this way by people who argue that children's folk psychology is not based on any theoretical knowledge. Second, the phrase is used to refer in a general way to children's folk psychological knowledge, a fairly loose use of the term "theory," which could be replaced by "conceptual system," for example. This use does not imply that children really are engaged in theory construction. However, the third way in which the phrase is used does take the idea of theory development seriously: children's theory development is seen to be analogous to theory development in science. This view is part of a general stance to think of cognitive development in terms of theory formation and theory change—as for example, Susan Carey, Annette Karmiloff-Smith, and Frank Keil have done in other domains.[17] This third position is the one that I am considering here as the Theory view. The psychologists' theory is that children develop a theory about the mind, which has led to designation of this view as the theory-theory—so good they named it twice, as Jim Russell put it.[18] To avoid confusion, I will call it the Theory view (capital "T") and I will refer to the child's theory of mind (small "t"). The Theory view, which I discussed in Chapter 8, is taken by Josef Perner, Henry Wellman, Alison Gopnik, John Flavell, and others. It is also my view, which has been implicit, and sometimes explicit, throughout the previous chapters. It focuses on the child's developing understanding of representation, of representational mental states.

According to the Theory view, concepts of mental states—of desire, intention, perception, belief, and so on—are theoretical entities. They are abstract and unobservable and are used to explain and predict observable human behavior. These theoretical concepts are at a different level than the observable phenomena, the actions and events that they explain. A theory is characterized by the coherence and interdependence of its concepts.

That is, the concepts work together, as in the system I described in Chapter 5—for example, people act in a way that will fulfill their desires, given their beliefs. Thus, the theory can interpret a wide range of evidence using a few concepts and laws.

A fundamental characteristic of any theory, whether that of child or scientist, is that it undergoes change. Theory construction has a developmental, dynamic nature. Theories are not static but are open to defeat by new evidence. Children do not go from a state of having no theory at all to having a fully fledged adultlike theory of mind; rather, they hold different theories at different stages. So it is better to talk about children's theories, rather than theory, of mind. It is a debatable question whether we should refer to the earlier theories as theories of *mind* or whether we should call them theories of behavior or theories of people. In any case, an important development occurs when children discover what the mind does, when they understand representational activity. This development may be characterized as a change from an earlier kind of theory of mind to a representational theory of mind,[19] or a change from a mentalistic theory of behavior to a theory of mind.[20] In either case, the critical achievement is an understanding of representation.

This change comes around four years of age. Three-year-olds understand the difference between thoughts and things, they understand that thoughts are unseen states. They have concepts of desire and perception, and they understand the causal links between what people want and what they do, for example, and between what people see and what they know (see Chapters 6 and 7). However, at this stage children see the relation between these mental entities and the world as direct.[21] They see thoughts as separate from the world and yet directly connected to the world, and so their predictions are based on these direct connections: they predict that someone who wants an object will look where the object is, for example. Some of their predictions will be disproved—children will be faced by people who act against their own desires by looking for things in the "wrong" places because they think they are somewhere else. Recently, Alison Gopnik and Henry Wellman have given a very clear description of the effects of such experience.[22] In general, they say, as evidence against a current theory accumulates it may be denied at first, then dealt with by ad hoc hypotheses, which may weigh the theory down, making it less elegant and simple. Then the whole system is reorganized into a new theory. Such is the case with the child's theory of mind.

At first, three-year-olds ignore even very strong counterevidence to their current theory. Remember the child in Chapter 8 who thought there was candy in the box and then expressed great surprise on finding it wasn't candy. When she was asked what she had thought was in the box before it was opened, she ignored the evidence of her own surprise and claimed she had said there were pencils in the box, even though less than an minute before she had said, "Smarties!" when she first saw the box, then "Holy moly, pencils!" when it was opened. An intermediate stage follows, Gopnik and Wellman say, during which children seem to be using two different theories, or rather, the old theory and some new hypotheses. For example, three-year-olds may be able to explain actions premised on false beliefs, even if they can't predict them.[23] That is, if they are forced to find an explanation for someone who frustrates her own desire by looking for something in the wrong place, they may be able to say she thinks that's where the object is. On the other hand, when they are asked where she will look, they are not faced with any discrepancy and predict she will look where she will find it, in the object's actual location. Finally, a new theory is formed, in which people do act to fulfill their desires but in the light of their beliefs. Minds are not seen as directly connected to the world; rather, the relation between the mind and the world is mediated by representation. Thus, children come to understand that people's thoughts are representations constructed by the mind, and that perceptions and beliefs represent the way the person takes the world to be, which is not necessarily the way it is.

Theories coherently organize many different types of evidence, but they are still specific to a particular domain. The development of the child's theory of mind goes on independent of the development of her theory of physics or of biology, for example. Some people have suggested that the child's construction of a theory in this particular domain reflects a more general change across domains, and that the child's development of an understanding of mind is one part of this larger picture.[24] The idea is that changes in children's general information-processing abilities—changes in memory or computational capacity, for example—are responsible for changes in their understanding of mind.[25]

Enculturation, Nativism, Simulation, Theory development, Domain-general development—how are we to decide among these alternative explanations? There is some sense in which each explanation provides part of the answer. I have expressed the view that children are developing a theory of mind, but other processes must also play significant roles. Theory formation, whether for children or scientists, always takes place within a particular culture, from which knowledge is acquired. And innate structures or abilities must be there at the beginning to provide a starting state that is later transformed by experience—the argument is really over how much is there and what kind of structure it is. Obviously information-processing abilities are also needed; without a certain memory capacity certain theories of mind might be impossible, for example.[26] Equally obviously, there can be no theoretical explanations without experience to explain, and such experience will include introspective evidence. Thus, all these processes are part of the cause, the debate concerns their relative importance. How do we decide that? What evidence do we have, or do we need to obtain, to support one view over another?

The Theory view predicts the development of concepts of different mental states at different ages, which are then applied to the self and to others. According to this view, the child uses her current theory to understand both her own mental experiences and those of other people. She understands the mental life of others just as well, or just as poorly, as she understands her own. This view would predict differences in a child's understanding of, say, desire and belief, but no difference between the child's understanding of each of these mental states in the self or in others. From a Simulation viewpoint the reverse is the case. Children simulate other people's experience by pretending to have the same mental state the other person has. The child is directly aware of her own beliefs and desires. She simulates the beliefs and desires of others. According to this view, we would expect children to understand their own mental states before they understand those of other people, but we would not expect a systematic difference between the child's understanding of different mental states within herself. Rather, we would expect the child to be equally aware of her own beliefs and desires and equally well able to introspect these different mental states.

As we saw in Chapter 8, the development of children's

ability to remember their own false beliefs parallels the development of their ability to predict another person's false belief. Alison Gopnik and Virginia Slaughter have investigated children's understanding of other kinds of their own mental states, such as desire, pretense, intention, and perception.[27] In each case, the children experienced a state, the state was changed, and they were asked about their original state. For example, a desire was satisfied, and so changed—the child wanted to read one of two books, that book was read to him, and then he said he desired the other one. Then he was asked, "When you first saw the books, before we read one, which one did you want?" Three-year-olds were much better at reporting their past and changed desires than their past and changed beliefs. Recall that three-year-olds also understand others' desires but not others' beliefs. The general order of difficulty for remembering these states was pretense and perception, then desire and intention, then belief, just the same order as understanding these states in others.

Thus, children understand their own mental states at the same age that they understand them in other people. The children's poor memory for their past beliefs cannot be a general problem of poor memory or lost access, because it is specific to beliefs and doesn't apply to desires, pretenses, and so on. These data seem to support the Theory view over the Simulation one. However, Paul Harris claims that the data do not refute the Simulation view. According to this view children introspect only their present mental states—and this they can do very well in Gopnik and Slaughter's tasks. In order to answer questions about their prior states, children have to run a simulation on their past self, just as on another person. Harris would argue that both the past belief and the past desire are recovered via simulation—in the desire case, the simulation is at a level that the three-year-old can achieve, but in the belief case, more default settings have to be altered, and so the task can't be achieved until four. However, one wonders why children need to simulate a state they have just experienced when they are well able to remember things that just happened a moment before, and so these data do appear to support the Theory view.

From a Theory point of view, it should be possible to accelerate the rate of development of a more advanced theory by providing children with salient evidence contradicting the theory they currently hold and favoring the new theory. For example, if a three-year-old is bombarded with examples of people being surprised and upset because they look for something they want in the place where they left it but from which it has been moved in their absence, will she develop an understanding of false belief sooner than a child who is not exposed to such experience? We do not know, since such an intervention study has not been performed. However, Josef Perner and his colleagues have found that children from larger families are more likely to perform successfully on false belief tasks, which they claim supports the Theory view of developing understanding of mind.[28] These children have more experience of intense social interaction with their siblings and therefore have a larger data base for developing a theory of mind, somewhat equivalent to being bombarded with examples in an intervention study. Perner also argues that these data argue against the Nativism or Domain-general development views, because it would be unlikely that children who happen to have more siblings undergo faster intellectual maturation.

Perhaps, however, the fact that children who experience more social interaction with siblings understand false belief sooner than those who don't supports the

Enculturation view. It may not be so much the experience of social interactions with their siblings that is important to children's precocious understanding of false belief, but their parents' explanations of these interactions—talk about who knew this, who thinks that, who wants what, and so on. We cannot decide between the alternative explanations on the basis of these data alone. As Peter Bryant has emphasized, there is no single perfect method for determining the cause of any development.[29] We need to combine methods. He argues that naturalistic observations over a period of time, plus an intervention study, provide a powerful combination. Judy Dunn's studies, which I have mentioned previously, demonstrate real-world relationships between, for example, the kind of talk children engage in with their family and their later understanding of false belief.[30] We do not know whether we could promote an understanding of false belief by exposing children to this kind of talk. Nevertheless, even without interventions, studies of individual differences are important because of their implications for different explanations of children's understanding of mind.

So far, research in theory of mind has focused on describing normative changes in children's understanding of various mental states. There has been little emphasis on individual differences in the time, rate, or manner of the development of this understanding, and little consideration given to what factors will predict children's success on theory of mind tasks. A few such studies are beginning to appear; I have already mentioned Dunn's and Perner's. Recently, Jenny Jenkins and I showed that false belief understanding is strongly associated with language ability, as is memory capacity, although that not independent of language ability.[31] Like Perner, we also found that children from larger families are more likely to pass false belief tasks even, as in our study, given equal language abilities. I think such studies will become more important in the next few years. A focus on individual differences and on longitudinal and intervention studies will provide important data in our quest to explain how children discover the mind. Relations between memory development and false belief understanding might be taken to support a Domain-general view, for example. Relations between children's imagination, shown in pretend play, and their understanding of others might support a Simulation view, and so on. Moreover, this focus on individual differences will lead us to think further about the significance of children's developing understanding of mind for their real-life relationships, about its consequences for children's social lives.

Consequences of Discovering the Mind

"Consequence" suggests both a temporal and a causal sequence: one thing follows another and one thing leads to another. The causal claim is the stronger claim and, as we have just seen, the one that is harder to establish. Here, I mean consequence in both senses. First, what follows in children's behavior after their discovery of the mind? Second, I imply that the discovery leads to these things. I do, however, acknowledge that we need more empirical work to establish the causal link. One piece of evidence that supports such a claim is the effect of deficit. One thing follows and leads to another—if the first is absent and the second doesn't appear, it strengthens the argument that the two are causally linked. This is one reason why investigation of autistic children's understanding of mind is so important. These children do not discover the mind in the normal way and their social relations and communicative abilities are severely impaired, which supports the argument that children's discovery of the mind underlies their ability to communicate and interact with others.

Certainly, social understanding and communicative competence are bound up with children's discovery of the mind, a point I have emphasized throughout the book. As children start to talk about people's thoughts, wants, feelings, and perceptions, they become able to share information with others, to show and tell them things. They become empathic; they understand what makes people sad and what will comfort them. They understand that people will be happy if they get what they want; later on they understand people will be happy if they think they are getting what they want or getting what they think they want. Understanding thoughts, wants, and feelings does not necessarily lead to altruism. Other factors come into play too. Such understanding can also be used for Machiavellian purposes—mental state understanding is needed to trick people and to lie to them, to hide things from them and to keep secrets from them. By five years of age children can do all of these things. They can be altruistic or Machiavellian, as we have seen. They are active participants in social exchanges with their friends and in their family life. What comes next? School comes next. For the next ten or even fifteen years, children spend five days a week, nine months of the year in school.

A long period of compulsory schooling is a recent Western invention. In previous centuries not all children went to school, nor do they now in some cultures. Ask any child why children go to school and invariably the response will be "to learn." There are ways of learning outside school, however. Apprenticeships come to mind. Here children (or adults) learn by being part of a purposeful activity. Apprentices watch and are given tasks to do that are part of the whole operation, easy ones at first and gradually more difficult ones. They are not told how to do the task, they imitate what they have seen others do. Do they need to understand the purpose to be able to perform? An open question. It seems likely that they need to understand that there is a purpose, that people have intentions, and this they will have understood from an early age. Understanding the particular purpose of the operation they are part of will presumably come gradually as they master its constituent tasks, even though they may never explicitly be told what this is. Unlike apprenticeship, schooling involves explicit instruction. How does children's discovery of the mind prepare them to learn in school?

Recently, Michael Tomasello and his colleagues have proposed a theory of human cultural learning in which the evolution of understanding of others' minds is related to the evolution of culture.[32] They conceive of the accumulation of culture as the product of cultural learning, a kind of learning dependent upon recognizing others' intentionality. They distinguish three levels of this recognition—of intention, of beliefs, and of beliefs about beliefs—and tie these three levels to three different forms of cultural learning—through imitation, instruction, and collaboration. Throughout this book we have seen how children come to recognize this intentionality, to understand themselves and other people as having intentions, beliefs, desires, hopes, fears, and so on. Part of this development is their understanding of people as cognitive beings who can think, learn, know, reason, and remember. I believe that such understanding determines in large part how children respond to the experience of schooling.

Ready for School

Children go to school to learn, we all agree on that, but how do they learn and how should they be taught? Here disagreement begins. There are two extreme views and the pendulum swings between them. At any one time, in any one school, the situation will be somewhere between these two extremes. On the traditional side, learning is absorbing, taking in what the teacher dispenses, presumably knowledge. Knowledge is seen as facts, which exist and which can be transmitted. According to this view, children are seen as ignorant, empty vessels to be filled with facts. On the other, progressive side, learning is constructing. Children construct knowledge through their own activity and experience. According to this view, children come to school with some understanding and beliefs about the world, although these beliefs may be mistaken and are open to change.[33]

This quick sketch of traditional and progressive philosophies of education is obviously a caricature. My concern here is with children's understanding of these things, in particular how their discovery of the mind informs this understanding. What do children need to do and to understand to be able to participate in these forms of education? Essentially, my argument is this: on the one hand, in the traditional system, the child needs social behaviors, whereas on the other, in the progressive system, she needs social understanding. This is rather cryptic and needs some elaboration. It relies on the distinction I made in Chapter 2 between first-order and second-order systems. Social behaviors are first-order, and social understandings are second-order. First-order systems have mental states, they have beliefs, desires, and intentions, as do second-order systems. However, beyond that, second-order systems have concepts of these mental states, they have beliefs about beliefs, and they can attribute beliefs and other mental states to themselves and others. Five-year-olds are second-order systems, as we have seen. My point is that traditional education does not capitalize on this, whereas progressive education does. That is to say, the school's philosophy of education, teachers' assumptions about children's minds, are just as important as the child's own beliefs.

I do not mean that in traditional systems children are passive, that they do not need to think. They do think: they think about the task and they think about the world. But they do not need to think about their thinking. In progressive systems children are seen as constructing their own knowledge. They need to understand what it is to know and how one comes to know. They do need to think about thinking. My argument is supported by studies of autistic children's educational experience, which show that they learn best in traditional settings. A systematic comparison of autistic children's progress in three different types of educational setting showed that they progressed best in a structured, didactic environment, and worst in one that was permissive and unstructured and placed more weight on the child's own activity.[34] Autistic children are not second-order systems, they do not think about minds, and they fare better under conditions that do not require them to do so.

Normally, by five children are second-order systems. By this age they have acquired concepts of a mind-independent reality and of people's beliefs about this reality. They recognize that different people may have different beliefs about the same reality and that beliefs are subject to change; this assumption is what makes discussion possible and valuable. They understand that people construct their knowledge through perception and communication, and that different information comes from different sensory modalities. They remember the source of their own beliefs. Indeed, as we have seen, five-year-olds already understand a great deal about thinking and learning in everyday social contexts.

In a progressive setting teachers acknowledge this and encourage children to make their understanding explicit by talking about it. Children need to think and talk about their thinking, and about their knowledge and learning. Such things are not directly observable but are made into objects of reflection through language. Even kindergarten children can be asked such questions as "Do you really know that or are you just guessing?" "Did you just think of that or did you remember it?" Vivian Paley's books show how well this can be done. For example, Paley writes about how she keeps track of the discussion at circle time, not to determine its direction, that comes from the children, but so that she and the children will understand how one thought leads to another. Paley's "keeping track" is rich in talk about thought. For example, "I *think* I *know* what *reminded* you of that, Deana . . ."[35] And the children's own production of talk about thoughts is encouraged by Paley's generous use of "why" questions:

Teacher: Why does Jack *decide* to climb the beanstalk?

Mary Anne: Maybe he *thinks* it's very cloudy up there and he doesn't *know* if there's a king or a giant there, so he just *wants to know*.[36]

In this way, by consciously introducing and using language about thinking in the classroom, teachers lead children to reflect on and to articulate their thinking and its expression. It may be that by explicitly ascribing a variety of mental states to children, the children will come to see themselves as holding these states. In Chapter 3 I said that parents treat babies' spontaneous noises and gestures as intentional communications and that within the context of this supportive system children learn to communicate. The baby reaches for his rattle and the mother treats it as a request for the rattle, maybe even saying, "Oh you want your rattle," or "Do you want your rattle?" and in time the child comes to request, not with a reach or not just with a reach, but with, "I want . . ." In the same way, in the classroom, if the teacher explicitly ascribes mental states of one kind or another to children, so they will come to see themselves as holding these states and come to talk that way themselves. Just as Paley said to Deana, "I think I know what *reminded* you of that," so Deana would come to see herself as reminded.

In Paley's classroom, the talk is not just about things in the world, it is also about the children's thoughts about things in the world. Here the class is planting lettuce seeds from a packet:

Eddie: . . . Anyway, how do we know it's really lettuce?

Teacher: The label says "Bibb Lettuce."

Eddie: What if it's really tomatoes?

Teacher: Oh. Are you *wondering* about the picture of tomatoes with the lettuce on the packet? It's just an idea for a salad, after the lettuce comes up.[37]

Eddie not only gets the answer to his question, he also gets to know that he was wondering. In another example, the children are going to act out a story, but first they'll talk about its various possible endings. Paley says, "We'll let the one who acts the part *decide* [what the ending will be] after we all give our *opinions*."[38] Thus the children know that their suggested endings are opinions, and the one who acts the part knows he has made a decision. The children's interest is in the story, but they are made aware of their thoughts about the story. In this way Paley capitalizes on the kindergarteners' second-order understanding and helps the children to articulate a variety of second-order states—*remindings, wonderings, decisions, opinions.*

We want to help children think and talk in this way, to reflect on their own and others' thoughts, so that the sophisticated social understanding they had as preschoolers of people as thinking beings will be carried over into the school context, where it will not only inform their understanding of how they think and learn in school but become more explicit and articulate. It is important to think of how we can best help children to acquire this way of thinking. This is an open question, one worth systematic study. My hunch is that if teachers talk the way Paley does about what they themselves *think, know, expect, remember, wonder about, have decided on, guessed,* and so on, and if they use these terms to describe and inquire about the child's thoughts, the children themselves will come to think and talk like this. Some evidence supports this hunch. Children whose mothers used more words like *know* and *think* when the children were two years old were themselves more likely to use these words at four years of age in their everyday talk and performed better in a test of their understanding of the distinction between knowing and thinking.[39]

Further support comes from the Robinsons' studies.[40] They were interested in children's ability to understand what has gone wrong when miscommunication occurs—has the speaker not been clear enough or has the listener misunderstood? In their task, the experimenter and the child each have an identical set of pictures, and there is a screen between them so that they can each see only their own set. The game is to pick a picture from your set and describe it so that the other person can pick the same one from his or her set. The pictures are designed so that an incomplete description will sometimes cause the partner to choose the wrong one. For example, if there are pictures of flowers, both big and small, red and blue, you need to specify both the size and the color to identify one uniquely. If you just say "red flower" you may have a big one and your partner may pick a small one. In this game, if an incomplete description was given and the partner picked one that didn't match, the child was asked what had gone wrong. At five children tended to blame the listener for choosing wrongly, whereas by seven they usually blamed the speaker for the faulty message.

Some of the children who were tested had been observed a few years earlier by Gordon Wells in a study of language development.[41] The Robinsons found a relation between the way mothers had queried the children's talk when the children were preschoolers and the children's performance on this task later on. If, say, the child made an unclear request, some mothers would talk just about the world: "Which one do you want, this or that?" whereas others would talk about the communication and about the world: "I don't understand. I don't know whether you want this one or that one." Of course, as we saw earlier, one cannot claim that the mothers' talk caused the children's better understanding of the communication game later on, but an intervention study helps support this argument.

The Robinsons played the communication game with preschoolers, and when incomplete descriptions were given, they responded in different ways to different groups of children, as the mothers had done. One group was told explicitly about their partners' uncertainty over picking the right card, for example, "I don't know which one you mean, you didn't tell me enough." Afterwards, the children in this group were better able than the other children to say who was responsible for the mistakes that were made when they watched another pair of people playing the game.

The results of these studies suggest that deliberately using talk about thought in the classroom will help children acquire this way of talking and thinking. It is not that children need to be taught lists of these words but that they need to come to think and to talk in this way by hearing them used appropriately. This is not to say that we shouldn't talk about the word itself when an occasion arises. For example, a group of first-grade children were measuring the length of parts of their body using popsicle sticks, but first they had to estimate how long they thought a part, their arm for example, would be, that is, how many popsicle sticks, and write that number in a column headed "guess."[42] Then they had to measure their arm and record the actual number of sticks in another column. Interestingly, if the children had guessed wrongly, they didn't like to leave that number in their book; they wanted to erase it and write the same number in both columns. Here was an ideal opportunity for the teacher to talk about the word *guess*, and about how guessing is different from knowing, to help the children think about their thinking.

Some time ago now, Margaret Donaldson showed us that children come to school well able to think and reason about the world in situations that make human sense to them.[43] What they have to learn to do in school is to think and reason in what she calls "disembedded contexts." Instead of dealing directly with the world in situations that make human sense, children have to use symbol systems and deal with representations of the world—in words and numbers, pictures and diagrams. Success in school depends on this ability. How can we help children to achieve it? At the beginning of their school career, Donaldson says, children's thinking is directed out at the world.

> What is going to be required for success in our educational system is that [the child] should learn to turn language and thought in upon themselves. He must become able to direct his own thought processes in a thoughtful manner. He must become able not just to talk but to choose what he will say, not just to interpret but to weigh possible interpretations. His conceptual system must expand in the direction of increasing ability to represent itself.[44]

She points out the importance of learning to read in giving children a reflective awareness of their language. However, that is not all that is required. Children also need a reflective awareness of their thought. In order to direct their own thought processes, children must become aware of them. This was Vygotsky's insight: "control of a function is the counterpart of one's consciousness of it . . . We use *consciousness* to denote awareness of the activity of the mind."[45] This is exactly what the child's discovery of the mind leads to—awareness of the mind's activity. And this is what is essential for success in school.

In Conclusion

In talking about the consequences of the child's discovery of the mind I have emphasized the consequences for schooling, for children's intellectual lives. Other consequences, those for their social lives, are just as important, as we have seen throughout the book. The understanding of minds that children acquire in the preschool years underlies their social interactions with family and friends and provides the foundation for their cognitive activities in school. School and family, cognition and affect, work and love—these remain of fundamental importance throughout our lives. It all begins with the child's discovery of the mind.

Notes

Suggested Reading

Index

Notes

1 / WHAT IS THE MIND?

1. P. M. Churchland, *Matter and Consciousness* (Cambridge, Mass.: MIT Press, 1984); S. Stich, *From Folk Psychology to Cognitive Science* (Cambridge, Mass.: Bradford Books/MIT Press, 1983).
2. D. Premack and G. Woodruff, "Does the Chimpanzee have a Theory of Mind?" *Behavioral and Brain Sciences* 1 (1978):515–526.
3. Ibid., p. 515.
4. Commentary on Premack and Woodruff, "Does the Chimpanzee Have a Theory of Mind?" *Behavioral and Brain Sciences* 1 (1978): J. Bennett, "Some Remarks about Concepts," pp. 557–560; D. C. Dennett, "Beliefs about Beliefs," pp. 568–570; G. Harman, "Studying the Chimpanzee's Theory of Mind," p. 591.
5. H. Wimmer and J. Perner, "Beliefs about Beliefs: Representation and Constraining Function of Wrong Beliefs in Young Children's Understanding of Deception," *Cognition* 13 (1983):103–128.
6. J. Piaget, *The Language and Thought of the Child* (London: Kegan Paul, 1926. Originally published in French in 1923); *Judgment and Reasoning in the Child* (London: Kegan Paul, 1928. Originally published in French in 1924); *The Child's Conception of the World* (London: Kegan Paul, 1929. Originally published in French in 1926); *The Child's Conception*

of Physical Causality (London: Kegan Paul, 1930. Originally published in French in 1927).

7. Piaget, *The Child's Conception of the World*, p. 94.
8. Ibid., p. 39.
9. Ibid., p. 55.
10 Ibid., p. 216.
11 Ibid., p. 176.
12 Piaget, *The Language and Thought of the Child*, p. 9.
13 J. Dunn, *The Beginnings of Social Understanding* (Cambridge, Mass.: Harvard University Press, 1988).
14 J. W. Astington and A. Gopnik, "Theoretical Explanations of Children's Understanding of the Mind," *British Journal of Developmental Psychology* 9 (1991):7–31.

2 / WHAT DOES THE MIND DO?

1. D. C. Dennett, *The Intentional Stance* (Cambridge, Mass.: Bradford Books/MIT Press, 1987).
2. F. Brentano, "The Distinction between Mental and Physical Phenomena," in *Realism and the Background of Phenomenology,* ed. R. M. Chisholm (New York: Free Press, 1960. Originally published in German in 1874), pp. 39–61.
3. J. Perner, *Understanding the Representational Mind* (Cambridge, Mass.: Bradford Books/MIT Press, 1991).
4. J. Perner, "On Representing That: The Asymmetry between Belief and Desire in Children's Theories of Mind," in *Children's Theories of Mind: Mental States and Social Understanding,* ed. D. Frye and C. Moore (Hillsdale, N.J.: Erlbaum, 1991), pp. 139–155.
5. R. D'Andrade, "A Folk Model of the Mind," in *Cultural Models in Language and Thought,* ed. D. Holland and N. Quinn (Cambridge: Cambridge University Press, 1987), pp. 112–148.
6. Perner, *Understanding the Representational Mind*, Chap. 2.
7. C. Darwin, *The Expression of the Emotions in Man and Animals* (London: Murray, 1872).
8. P. Ekman and W. Freisen, "Constants across Cultures in

the Face and Emotion," *Journal of Personality and Social Psychology* 117 (1972):124–129.

9. P. L. Harris, *Children and Emotion: The Development of Psychological Understanding* (Oxford: Basil Blackwell, 1989).

10. C. Lutz, "Goals, Events, and Understanding in Ifaluk Emotion Theory," in *Cultural Models in Language and Thought,* ed. Holland and Quinn, pp. 290–312.

11. Harris, *Children and Emotion.*

12. A. Lock, "Universals in Human Conception," and P. Heelas, "The Model Applied: Anthropology and Indigenous Psychologies," in *Indigenous psychologies,* ed. P. Heelas and A. Lock (London: Academic Press, 1981), pp. 19–36 and pp. 39–63.

13. J. Dunn, *The Beginnings of Social Understanding* (Cambridge, Mass.: Harvard University Press, 1988), p. 33.

14. C. Linde, "Explanatory Systems in Oral Life Stories," in *Cultural Models in Language and Thought,* ed. Holland and Quinn, pp. 343–366.

15. Heelas, "The Model Applied."

16. M. Cole and S. R. Cole, *The Development of Children* (New York: Scientific American Books, 1989).

3 / PEOPLE AND THINGS

1. D. N. Stern, *The Interpersonal World of the Infant* (New York: Basic Books, 1985).

2. T. Field, *Infancy,* (Cambridge, Mass.: Harvard University Press, 1990).

3. C. A. Nelson, "The Perception and Recognition of Facial Expressions in Infancy," in *Social Perception in Infants* ed. T. M. Field and N. A. Fox (Norwood, N.J.: Ablex, 1985), pp. 101–125.

4. M. D. Klinnert, J. J. Campos, J. F. Sorce, R. N. Emde, and M. Svenjda, "Emotions as Behavior Regulators: Social Referencing in Infancy," in *Emotion: Theory, Research, and Experience, vol. 2: Emotions in Early Development,* eds. R. Plutchik and H. Kellerman (New York: Academic Press, 1983), pp. 57–86.

5. M. Scaife and J. S. Bruner, "The Capacity for Joint Visual Attention in the Infant," *Nature* 253 (1975):265–266.

6. G. Butterworth, "The Ontogeny and Phylogeny of Joint Visual Attention," in *Natural Theories of Mind: Evolution, Development and Simulation of Everyday Mindreading*, ed. A. Whiten (Oxford: Basil Blackwell, 1991), pp. 223–232.

7. H. R. Schaffer, *The Child's Entry into a Social World* (London: Academic Press, 1984). See especially Chap. 4, "Face-to-face Interactions."

8. C. Trevarthen, "The Foundations of Intersubjectivity: Development of Interpersonal and Cooperative Understanding in Infants," in *The Social Foundations of Language and Thought*, ed. D. R. Olson (New York: Norton, 1980), pp. 316–342.

9. G. A. Miller and P. N. Johnson-Laird, *Language and Perception* (Cambridge, Mass.: Harvard University Press, 1976).

10. P. A. de Villiers and J. G. de Villiers, *Early Language* (Cambridge, Mass.: Harvard University Press, 1979).

11. J. Lyons, *Noam Chomsky*, rev. ed. (Harmondsworth, England: Penguin, 1977).

12. J. S. Bruner, "The Ontogenesis of Speech Acts," *Journal of Child Language* 2 (1975):1–19; E. Bates, *Language and Context: The Acquisition of Pragmatics* (New York: Academic Press, 1976).

13. J. Bruner, *Child's Talk: Learning to Use Language* (Oxford: Oxford University Press, 1983).

14. A. Lock, *The Guided Reinvention of Language* (London: Academic Press, 1980).

15. A. L. Carter, "From Sensori-motor Vocalizations to Words: A Case Study of Attention-directing Communication in the Second Year," in *Action, Gesture and Symbol: The Emergence of Language*, ed. A. Lock (London: Academic Press, 1978), pp. 310–349.

16. H. P. Grice, "Meaning," *Philosophical Review* 66 (1957):377–388.

17. Bruner, *Child's Talk.*

18. I. Bretherton, S. McNew, and M. Beeghly-Smith, "Early Person Knowledge as Expressed in Gestural and Verbal

Communication: When Do Infants Acquire a 'Theory of Mind'?" in *Infant Social Cognition*, ed. M. E. Lamb and L. R. Sherod (Hillsdale, N.J.: Erlbaum, 1981), pp. 333–373.

19. E. Winner, *The Point of Words: Children's Understanding of Metaphor and Irony* (Cambridge, Mass.: Harvard University Press, 1988).

20. M. Donaldson, *Children's Minds* (Glasgow: Fontana/Collins, 1978), p. 37.

4 / THOUGHTS AND THINGS

1. J. Piaget, *The Origins of Intelligence in Children* (London: Kegan Paul, 1936. Originally published in French in 1936); *The Construction of Reality in the Child* (New York: Basic Books, 1954. Originally published in French in 1937).

2. K. Nelson, "Monologue as Representation of Real-life Experience," in *Narratives from the Crib*, (pp. 27–72), ed. K. Nelson (Cambridge, Mass.: Harvard University Press, 1989), p. 64.

3. A. Gopnik, "Words and Plans: Early Language and the Development of Intelligent Action," *Journal of Child Language* 9 (1982):303–318.

4. J. Piaget, *Play, Dreams and Imitation in Childhood* (New York, Norton, 1962. Originally published in French in 1945).

5. Ibid., p. 97.

6. C. Garvey, *Play* (Cambridge, Mass.: Harvard University Press, 1977), pp. 96–100.

7. D. P. Wolf, J. Rygh, and J. Altshuler, "Agency and Experience: Actions and States in Play Narratives," in *Symbolic Play: The Development of Social Understanding* (pp. 195–217), ed. I. Bretherton (Orlando, Fla.: Academic Press, 1984), pp. 196–197.

8. Garvey, *Play*.

9. J. Dunn and N. Dale, "I a Daddy: 2-year-olds' Collaboration in Joint Play with Sibling and Mother," in *Symbolic Play* (pp. 131–158), ed. Bretherton, p. 142.

10. I. Bretherton, S. McNew, and M. Beeghly-Smith, "Early Person Knowledge as Expressed in Gestural and Verbal

Communication: When Do Infants Acquire a 'Theory of Mind'?" in *Infant Social Cognition*, ed. M. E. Lamb and L. R. Sherod (Hillsdale, N.J.: Erlbaum, 1981), pp. 333–373; I. Bretherton and M. Beeghly, "Talking about Internal States: The Acquisition of an Explicit Theory of Mind," *Developmental Psychology* 6 (1982):906–921.

11. P. L. Harris and R. D. Kavanaugh, "Young Children's Understanding of Pretense," *Monographs of the Society for Research in Child Development* 58 (1993, 1, Serial No. 231).

12. A. M. Leslie, "Some Implications of Pretense for Mechanisms Underlying the Child's Theory of Mind," in *Developing Theories of Mind*, ed. J. W. Astington, P. L. Harris, and D. R. Olson (New York: Cambridge University Press, 1988), pp. 19–46.

13. Ibid., p. 22.

14. A. M. Leslie, "The Theory of Mind Impairment in Autism: Evidence for a Modular Mechanism of Development?" in *Natural Theories of Mind: Evolution, Development and Simulation of Everyday Mindreading*, ed. A. Whiten (Oxford: Basil Blackwell, 1991), pp. 63–78.

15. Piaget, *Play, Dreams and Imitation*, p. 96.

16. L. Bloom, M. Rispola, B. Gartner, and J. Hafitz, "Acquisition of Complementation," *Journal of Child Language* 16 (1989):101–120.

17. J. Perner, *Understanding the Representational Mind* (Cambridge, Mass.: Bradford Books/MIT Press, 1991).

18. A. S. Lillard, "Pretend Play Skills and the Child's Theory of Mind," *Child Development* 64 (1993): 348–371.

19. Harris and Kavanaugh, "Young Children's Understanding of Pretense," p. 78.

20. H. M. Wellman and A. K. Hickling, "Understanding Pretense as Pretense: Commentary on Harris and Kavanaugh," *Monographs of the Society for Research in Child Development* 58 (1993, 1, Serial No. 231).

21. H. M. Wellman, *The Child's Theory of Mind* (Cambridge, Mass.: Bradford Books/MIT Press, 1990).

22. L. Forguson and A. Gopnik, "The Ontogeny of Common

Sense," in *Developing Theories of Mind*, ed. Astington et al., pp. 226–243.

23. J. Piaget, *The Child's Conception of the World* (London: Kegan Paul, 1929. Originally published in French in 1926), p. 55.

24. Perner, *Understanding the Representational Mind*, pp. 174–176.

25. C. Garvey and R. Berndt, "Organization of Pretend Play," *JSAS Catalog of Selected Documents in Psychology* (Ms. No. 1589) 7 (1977), p. 4.

26. J. and E. Newson, *Four Years Old in an Urban Community* (Harmondsworth, England: Penguin, 1970).

27. Ibid., p. 185.

28. Ibid.

29. P. L. Harris, E. Brown, C. Marriott, S. Whittall, and S. Harmer, "Monsters, Ghosts and Witches: Testing the Limits of the Fantasy-reality Distinction in Young Children," *British Journal of Developmental Psychology* 9 (1991):105–123.

30. Ibid., p. 105.

5 / THOUGHT AND LANGUAGE

1. C. N. Johnson and H. M. Wellman, "Children's Developing Conceptions of the Mind and Brain," *Child Development* 53 (1982):222–234. (Note: Three-year-olds were unsuccessful at these tasks, perhaps indicating, as I suggested in Chapter 2, that at first children may not understand representational activity even though they know something about representations.)

2. J. A. Fodor, "Fodor's Guide to Mental Representation: The Intelligent Auntie's Vade-mecum," *Mind* 94 (1985):76–100.

3. J. W. Astington and D. R. Olson, "Metacognitive and Metalinguistic Language: Learning to Talk about Thought," *Applied Psychology: An International Review* 39 (1990):77–87.

4. J. R. Searle, *Speech Acts: An Essay in the Philosophy of Language* (Cambridge: Cambridge University Press, 1969).

5. J. L. Austin, *How to Do Things with Words* (Cambridge, Mass.: Harvard University Press, 1962).
6. M. Donaldson, *Children's Minds* (Glasgow: Fontana/Collins, 1978).
7. J. W. Astington, "Promises: Words or Deeds?" *First Language* 8 (1988):259–270.
8. J. Perner, *Understanding the Representational Mind* (Cambridge, Mass.: Bradford Books/MIT Press, 1991), p. 107.
9. This is what John Searle refers to as the causal selfreferentiality of intention. J. R. Searle, *Intentionality: An Essay in the Philosophy of Mind* (Cambridge: Cambridge University Press, 1983), pp. 85–86.
10. Henry Wellman's is the best description I know and I recommend it to fill out the one given here. H. M. Wellman, *The Child's Theory of Mind* (Cambridge, Mass.: Bradford Books/MIT Press, 1990), especially Chap. 4.

6 / THINKING ABOUT WANTING

1. P. L. Harris, C. N. Johnson, D. Hutton, G. Andrews and T. Cooke, "Young Children's Theory of Mind and Emotion," *Cognition and Emotion* 3 (1989):379–400.
2. L. Forguson, *Common Sense* (London: Routledge, 1989).
3. K. Bartsch and H. M. Wellman, *Children Talk about the Mind* (New York: Oxford University Press, in press).
4. H. M. Wellman, "From Desires to Beliefs: Acquisition of a Theory of Mind," in *Natural Theories of Mind: Evolution, Development and Simulation of Everyday Mindreading* (pp. 19–38), ed. A. Whiten (Oxford: Basil Blackwell, 1991), p. 34.
5. Ibid., p. 35.
6. D. Ridgeway, E. Waters, and S. A. Kuczaj, "Acquisition of Emotion-descriptive Language: Receptive and Productive Vocabulary Norms for Ages 18 Months to 6 Years," *Developmental Psychology* 21 (1985):901–908.
7. I. Bretherton and M. Beeghly, "Talking about Internal States: The Acquisition of an Explicit Theory of Mind," *Developmental Psychology* 18 (1982):906–921.

8. J. Dunn, I. Bretherton, and P. Munn, "Conversations about Feeling States between Mothers and Their Young Children," *Developmental Psychology* 23 (1987):132–139.

9. P. Smiley and J. Huttenlocher, "Young Children's Acquisition of Emotion Concepts," in *Children's Understanding of Emotion*, ed. C. Saarni and P. L. Harris (Cambridge: Cambridge University Press, 1989), pp. 27–49.

10. H. M. Wellman, P. L. Harris, M. Banerjee, and A. Sinclair, "Early Understandings of Emotion: Evidence from Natural Language" *Cognition and Emotion* (in press).

11. D. P. Wolf, J. Rygh, and J. Altshuler, "Agency and Experience: Actions and States in Play Narratives," in *Symbolic Play: The Development of Social Understanding* (pp. 195–217), ed. I. Bretherton (Orlando, Fla.: Academic Press, 1984), p. 202.

12. J. Dunn, J. Brown, and L. Beardsall, "Family Talk about Feeling States and Children's Later Understanding of Others' Emotions," *Developmental Psychology* 27 (1991):448–455.

13. H. M. Wellman, *The Child's Theory of Mind* (Cambridge, Mass.: Bradford Books/MIT Press, 1990), Chap. 8.

14. G. G. Fein, "The Self-building Potential of Pretend Play, or 'I Got a Fish, All by Myself,'" in *Becoming a Person* (pp. 328–346), ed. M. Woodhead, R. Carr, and P. Light (London: Routledge, 1991), pp. 333–334.

15. J. Dunn, "Young Children's Understanding of Other People: Evidence from Observations within the Family," in *Children's Theories of Mind* (pp. 97–114), ed. D. Frye and C. Moore (Hillsdale, N.J.: Erlbaum, 1991), p. 101.

16. Ibid., pp. 101–102.

17. J. Piaget, *The Moral Judgement of the Child* (Harmondsworth, England: Penguin, 1977. First published in French in 1932), p. 175.

18. T. R. Shultz, "Development of the Concept of Intention," in *Minnesota Symposium on Child Psychology*, vol. 13 (pp. 131–164), ed. W. A. Collins (Hillsdale, N.J.: Erlbaum, 1980), p. 157.

19. R. Brown, *A First Language: The Early Stages* (Cambridge, Mass.: Harvard University Press, 1973), p. 318.
20. Shultz, "Development of the Concept of Intention."
21. J. W. Astington and A. Gopnik, "Developing Understanding of Desire and Intention," in *Natural Theories of Mind*, ed. Whiten. pp. 39–50.
22. E. Lee, "Young Children's Understanding of Intention" (doctoral dissertation, Ontario Institute for Studies in Education, in preparation).
23. J. W. Astington, "Intention in the Child's Theory of Mind," in *Children's Theories of Mind*, ed. Frye and Moore, pp. 157–172.
24. L. Moses, "Young Children's Understanding of Intention and Belief" (doctoral dissertation, Stanford University, 1990).
25. J. R. Searle, *Intentionality: An Essay in the Philosophy of Mind* (Cambridge: Cambridge University Press, 1983), p. 82.
26. J. W. Astington and E. Lee, "What Do Children Know about Intentional Causation?" (Paper presented at the Biennial Meeting of the Society for Research in Child Development, Seattle, Wash., April 1991).
27. J. Perner, *Understanding the Representational Mind* (Cambridge, Mass.: Bradford Books/MIT Press, 1991), pp. 224–226.

7 / THINKING ABOUT KNOWING

1. J. Peskin, "Ruse and Representations: On Children's Ability to Conceal Information," *Developmental Psychology* 28 (1992):84–89.
2. P. M. Greenfield, "Toward an Operational and Logical Analysis of Intentionality: The Use of Discourse in Early Child Language," in *The Social Foundations of Language and Thought* (pp. 254–279), ed. D. R. Olson (New York: Norton, 1980) p. 275.
3. M. Scaife and J. S. Bruner, "The Capacity for Joint Visual Attention in the Human Infant," *Nature* 253 (1975):265–266. G. Butterworth, "The Ontogeny and Phylogeny of Joint Visual Attention," in *Natural Theories of Mind: Evolu-*

tion, Development and Simulation of Everyday Mindreading,
ed. A. Whiten (Oxford: Basil Blackwell, 1991), pp. 223–232.

4. I. Bretherton, S. McNew, and M. Beeghly-Smith, "Early
Person Knowledge as Expressed in Gestural and Verbal
Communication: When Do Infants Acquire a 'Theory of
Mind'?" in *Infant Social Cognition,* ed. M. E. Lamb and L.
R. Sherod (Hillsdale N.J.: Erlbaum, 1981), pp. 333–373.

5. S. Baron-Cohen, "Precursors to a Theory of Mind: Understanding Attention in Others," in *Natural Theories of Mind:
Evolution, Development and Simulation of Everyday Mindreading,* ed. A. Whiten (Oxford: Basil Blackwell, 1991), pp. 233–
251.

6. J. Perner, *Understanding the Representational Mind* (Cambridge, Mass.: Bradford Books/MIT Press, 1991), p. 131.

7. J. D. Lempers, E. R. Flavell, and J. H. Flavell, "The Development in Very Young Children of Tacit Knowledge Concerning Visual Perception," *Genetic Psychology Monographs*
95 (1977):3–53.

8. Perner, *Understanding the Representational Mind,* p. 140.

9. C. Pratt and P. E. Bryant,"Young Children Understand that
Looking Leads to Knowing (So Long as They Are Looking
into a Single Barrel)," *Child Development* 61 (1990):973–982;
B. H. Pillow, "Early Understanding of Perception as a
Source of Knowledge," *Journal of Experimental Child Psy-
chology* 47 (1989):116–129.

10. J. H. Flavell, B. A. Everett, K. Croft, and E. R. Flavell,
"Young Children's Knowledge about Visual Perception:
Further Evidence for the Level 1-Level 2 Distinction," *De-
velopmental Psychology* 17 (1981):99–103.

11. Ibid. See also Z. S. Masangkay, K. A. McCluskey, C.W.
McIntyre, J. Sims-Knight, B. E. Vaughn, and J. H. Flavell,
"The Early Development of Inferences about the Visual
Percepts of Others," *Child Development* 45 (1974):357–366.

12. J. H. Flavell, "The Development of Children's Knowledge
about the Mind: From Cognitive Connections to Mental
Representations," in *Developing Theories of Mind,* ed. J. W.
Astington, P. L. Harris, and D. R. Olson (New York: Cambridge University Press, 1988), pp. 244–267.

13. T. K. Ruffman, D. R. Olson, and J. W. Astington, "Chil-

dren's Understanding of Visual Ambiguity," *British Journal of Developmental Psychology* 9 (1991):89–102.

14. A. Gopnik and P. Graf, "Knowing How You Know: Young Children's Ability to Identify and Remember the Sources of Their Beliefs," *Child Development* 59 (1988):1366–1371; D. K. O'Neill and A. Gopnik, "Young Children's Ability to Identify the Sources of Their Beliefs," *Developmental Psychology* 27 (1991):390–397.

15. D. K. O'Neill, J. W. Astington, and J. H. Flavell, "Young Children's Understanding of the Role Sensory Experiences Play in Knowledge Acquisition," *Child Development* 63 (1992):474–490.

16. Perner, *Understanding the Representational Mind,* p. 153; H. M. Wellman, *The Child's Theory of Mind* (Cambridge, Mass.: Bradford Books/MIT Press, 1990), pp. 283–284.

17. Perner, *Understanding the Representational Mind,* p. 153.

18. K. Bartsch and H. M. Wellman, *Children Talk about the Mind* (New York: Oxford University Press, in press).

19. H. M. Wellman, "From Desires to Beliefs: Acquisition of a Theory of Mind," in *Natural Theories of Mind: Evolution, Development and Simulation of Everyday Mindreading* (pp. 19–38), ed. A. Whiten (Oxford: Basil Blackwell, 1991), p. 34.

20. Ibid., p. 35.

21. Perner, *Understanding the Representational Mind,* Chap. 7.

22. I thank Marion Herman for this anecdote.

23. A. A. Aksu-Koç, *The Acquisition of Aspect and Modality: The Case of Past Reference in Turkish* (Cambridge: Cambridge University Press, 1988).

8 / THINKING ABOUT BELIEVING

1. M. Shatz, H. M. Wellman, and S. Silber, "The Acquisition of Mental Verbs: A Systematic Investigation of the First Reference to Mental State," *Cognition* 14 (1983):301–321; p. 308.

2. Ibid.

3. K. Bartsch and H. M. Wellman, *Children Talk about the Mind* (New York: Oxford University Press, in press).

4. D. Premack and G. Woodruff, "Does the Chimpanzee Have a Theory of Mind?" *Behavioral and Brain Sciences* 1 (1978):515–526.

5. Commentary on Premack and Woodruff, "Does the Chimpanzee have a Theory of Mind?" *Behavioral and Brain Sciences* 1 (1978): J. Bennett, "Some Remarks about Concepts," pp. 557–560; D. C. Dennett, "Beliefs about Beliefs." pp. 568–570; G. Harman, "Studying the Chimpanzee's Theory of Mind," p. 591.

6. Dennett, "Beliefs about Beliefs," p. 569 (italics in original).

7. J. Perner, S. Leekam, and H. Wimmer, "Three-year-olds' Difficulty with False Belief: The Case for a Conceptual Deficit," *British Journal of Developmental Psychology* 5 (1987):125–137; H. Wimmer and J. Perner, "Beliefs about Beliefs: Representation and Constraining Function of Wrong Beliefs in Young Children's Understanding of Deception," *Cognition* 13 (1983):103–128.

8. L. J. Moses and J. H. Flavell, "Inferring False Beliefs from Actions and Reactions," *Child Development* 61 (1990):929–945.

9. Perner et al., "Three-year-olds' Difficulty with False Belief."

10. A. Gopnik and J. W. Astington, "Children's Understanding of Representational Change and its Relation to Their Understanding of False Belief and the Appearance-reality Distinction," *Child Development* 58 (1988):26–37.

11. J. W. Astington and A. Gopnik, "Knowing You've Changed Your Mind: Children's Understanding of Representational Change," in *Developing Theories of Mind* (pp. 193–206), ed. J. W. Astington, P. L. Harris, and D. R. Olson (New York: Cambridge University Press, 1988), p. 195.

12. H. Wimmer and M. Hartl, "Against the Cartesian View on Mind: Young Children's Difficulty with Own False Beliefs," *British Journal of Developmental Psychology* 9 (1991):125–138.

13. Ibid.

14. Astington and Gopnik, "Knowing You've Changed Your Mind."

15. J. H. Flavell, F. L. Green, and E. R. Flavell, "Development of Knowledge about the Appearance-reality Distinction," *Monographs of the Society for Research in Child Development* 51 (1986, 1, Serial No. 212).

16. J. W. Astington and A. Gopnik, "Theoretical Explanations of Children's Understanding of the Mind," *British Journal of Developmental Psychology* 9 (1991):7–31.

17. Ibid.

18. H. M. Wellman and K. Bartsch, "Young Children's Reasoning about Beliefs," *Cognition* 30 (1988):239–277.

19. D. Zaitchik, "Is Only Seeing Really Believing?: Sources of True Belief in the False Belief Task," *Cognitive Development* 6 (1991) 91–103.

20. M. Siegal and K. Beattie, "Where to Look First for Children's Knowledge of False Belief," *Cognition* 38 (1991):1–12.

21. P. Mitchell and H. Lacohée, "Children's Early Understanding of False Belief," *Cognition* 39 (1991):107–127.

22. Gopnik and Astington, "Children's Understanding of Representational Change."

23. C. Moore, K. Pure, and D. Furrow, "Children's Understanding of the Modal Expressions of Speaker Certainty and Uncertainty and its Relation to the Development of a Representational Theory of Mind," *Child Development* 61 (1990):722–730.

24. Ibid.

25. Flavell et al., "Development of Knowledge about the Appearance-reality Distinction."

26. J. H. Flavell, "The Development of Children's Knowledge about the Mind: From Cognitive Connections to Mental Representations," in *Developing Theories of Mind*, ed. Astington et al. pp. 244–267; A. Gopnik, "Developing the Idea of Intentionality: Children's Theories of Mind," *Canadian Journal of Philosophy* 20 (1990):89–114; D. R. Olson, "Making Up Your Mind," *Canadian Psychology* 30 (1989):617–627; J. Perner, *Understanding the Representational Mind* (Cam-

bridge, Mass.: Bradford Books/MIT Press, 1991); H. M. Wellman, *The Child's Theory of Mind* (Cambridge, Mass.: Bradford Books/MIT Press, 1990).

27. N. Goodman, *Languages of Art* (Indianapolis: Hackett, 1976).
28. J. H. Flavell, X-D. Zhang, H. Zou, Q. Dong, and S. Qi, "A Comparison between the Development of the Appearance-reality Distinction in the People's Republic of China and the United States," *Cognitive Psychology* 15 (1983):459–466.
29. P. L. Harris and D. Gross, "Children's Understanding of Real and Apparent Emotion," in *Developing Theories of Mind*, ed. Astington et al. pp. 295–314.
30. D. Gardner, P. L. Harris, M. Ohmoto, and T. Hamasaki, "Japanese Children's Understanding of the Distinction between Real and Apparent Emotion," *International Journal of Behavioral Development* 11 (1988):203–218.
31. J. Avis and P. L. Harris, "Belief-desire Reasoning among Baka Children: Evidence for a Universal Conception of Mind," *Child Development* 62 (1991):460–467.
32. P. McCormick, "Intentionality and Language: Is Belief Possible without the Language of Belief?" *Periodically . . . Newsletter of the McLuhan Program in Culture and Technology, University of Toronto* 12 (1989):4–5.
33. P. McCormick, "Quechua Children's Theory of Mind" (Paper presented at the Sixth University of Waterloo Conference on Child Development, Waterloo, Ontario, May 1990).
34. M. E. Vasek, "Lying as a Skill: The Development of Deception in Children," in *Deception: Perspectives on Human and Non-human Deceit* (pp. 271–292), ed. R. W. Mitchell & N. S. Thompson (New York: SUNY Press, 1986), p. 286.
35. See J. Dunn, *The Beginnings of Social Understanding* (Cambridge, Mass.: Harvard University Press, 1988).
36. Ibid., p. 21.
37. Perner, *Understanding the Representational Mind*, pp. 191–193.
38. M. Stouthamer-Loeber, "Young Children's Verbal Misrep-

resentations of Reality," in *Children's Interpersonal Trust*, ed. K. Rotenberg (New York: Springer-Verlag, 1991), pp. 20–42.

39. J. Piaget, *The Moral Judgement of the Child* (Harmondsworth, England: Penguin, 1977. Originally published in French in 1932).

40. H. Wimmer, S. Gruber, and J. Perner, "Young Children's Conception of Lying: Lexical Realism—Moral Subjectivism," *Journal of Experimental Child Psychology* 37 (1984):1–30.

41. Stouthamer-Loeber, "Young Children's Verbal Misrepresentations of Reality."

42. L. Coleman and P. Kay, "Prototype Semantics: The English Word *Lie*," *Language* 57 (1981):26–44.

43. S. R. Leekam, "Jokes and Lies: Children's Understanding of Intentional Falsehood," in *Natural Theories of Mind: Evolution, Development and Simulation of Everyday Mindreading*, ed. A. Whiten (Oxford: Basil Blackwell, 1991), pp. 159–174.

44. E. Winner, *The Point of Words* (Cambridge, Mass.: Harvard University Press, 1988).

45. M. J. Chandler, A. S. Fritz, and S. M. Hala, "Small Scale Deceit: Deception as a Marker of 2-, 3- and 4-year-olds' Early Theories of Mind," *Child Development* 60 (1989):1263–1277.

46. B. Sodian, "The Development of Deception in Young Children," *British Journal of Developmental Psychology* 9 (1991):173–188.

47. J. Russell, N. Mauthner, S. Sharpe, and T. Tidswell, "The 'Windows Task' as a Measure of Strategic Deception in Preschoolers and Autistic Subjects," *British Journal of Developmental Psychology* 9 (1991):331–349.

48. J. Peskin, "Ruse and Representations: On Children's Ability to Conceal Information," *Developmental Psychology* 28 (1992):84–89.

49. Chandler, Fritz, and Hala, "Small Scale Deceit."

50. S. Hala, M. Chandler, and A. S. Fritz, "Fledgling Theories of Mind: Deception as a Marker of 3-year-olds' Under-

standing of False Belief," *Child Development* 62 (1991):83–97.

51. B. Sodian, C. Taylor, P. L. Harris, and J. Perner, "Early Deception and the Child's Theory of Mind: False Trails and Genuine Markers," *Child Development* 62 (1991):468–483; J. R. Speer, G. M. Sullivan, and N. Smith, "Hiding Paradigm Affords No Evidence of Deceptive Intent in 2 1/2-year-olds" (Paper presented at the Annual Meeting of the American Psychological Society, San Diego, Calif., June 1992).

52. S. R. Leekam, "Believing and Deceiving: Steps to Becoming a Good Liar," in *Cognitive and Social Factors in Early Deception*, ed. S. J. Ceci, M. D. Leichtman, and M. E. Putnick (Hillsdale, N.J.: Erlbaum, 1992), pp. 47–62.

53. Rotenberg, *Children's Interpersonal Trust*.

9 / THE UNDISCOVERED MIND

1. C. C. Park, *The Siege: The First Eight Years of an Autistic Child*, 2d ed., with an epilogue, "Fifteen Years Later." (Boston, Mass.: Little, Brown, 1982).

2. Ibid., p. 6.

3. Ibid., p. 28.

4. Ibid., p. 29.

5. Ibid., p. 74.

6. L. Kanner, "Autistic Disturbances of Affective Contact," *Nervous Child* 2 (1943):217–150.

7. N. O'Connor and B. Hermelin, "Autism," in *The Oxford Companion to the Mind*, ed. R. L. Gregory and O. L. Zangwill (Oxford: Oxford University Press, 1987), pp. 63–65.

8. U. Frith, *Autism: Explaining the Enigma* (Oxford: Basil Blackwell, 1989), pp. 64–67.

9. A. Lovell, *In a Summer Garment: The Experience of an Autistic Child* (London: Secker & Warburg, 1978), p. 1.

10. It is also the case that the reverse may be true, children who have severe mental impairments may not be socially impaired. See L. Wing and J. Gould, "Severe Impairments

of Social Interaction and Associated Abnormalities in Children: Epidemiology and Classification," *Journal of Autism and Developmental Disorders* 9 (1979):11–30.

11. S. Folstein and M. Rutter, "Infantile Autism: A Genetic Study of 21 Twin Pairs," *Journal of Child Psychology and Psychiatry* 18 (1977):297–321.

12. S. Baron-Cohen, A. M. Leslie, and U. Frith, "Mechanical, Behavioural and Intentional Understanding of Picture Stories in Autistic Children," *British Journal of Developmental Psychology* 4 (1986):113–125.

13. H. Wimmer and J. Perner, "Beliefs about Beliefs: Representation and Constraining Function of Wrong Beliefs in Young Children's Understanding of Deception," *Cognition* 13 (1983):103–128.

14. S. Baron-Cohen, A. M. Leslie, and U. Frith, "Does the Autistic Child Have a 'Theory of Mind'?" *Cognition* 21 (1985):37–46.

15. A. M. Leslie and U. Frith, "Autistic Children's Understanding of Seeing, Knowing and Believing," *British Journal of Developmental Psychology* 6 (1988):315–324.

16. J. Perner, U. Frith, A. M. Leslie, and S. R. Leekam, "Exploration of the Autistic Child's Theory of Mind: Knowledge, Belief, and Communication," *Child Development* 60 (1989):689–700.

17. B. Sodian and U. Frith, "The Theory of Mind Deficit in Autism: Evidence from Deception," in *Understanding Other Minds: Perspectives from Autism,* ed. S. Baron-Cohen, H. Tager-Flusberg and D. Cohen (Oxford: Oxford University Press, 1993), pp. 158–180.

18. J. Russell, N. Mauthner, S. Sharpe, and T. Tidswell, "The 'Windows Task' as a Measure of Strategic Deception in Preschoolers and Autistic Subjects," *British Journal of Development Psychology* 9 (1991):331–349.

19. S. Baron-Cohen, "Are Autistic Children 'Behaviorists'? An Examination of Their Mental-physical and Appearance-reality Distinctions," *Journal of Autism and Developmental Disorders* 19 (1989):579–600.

20. S. Baron-Cohen, "The Development of a Theory of Mind in Autism: Deviance and Delay?" *Psychiatric Clinics of North America* 14 (1991):33–51.
21. H. Tager-Flusberg, "Autistic Children's Talk about Psychological States: Deficits in the Early Acquisition of a Theory of Mind," *Child Development* 63 (1992):161–172.
22. S. Baron-Cohen, "Autism and Symbolic Play," *British Journal of Developmental Psychology* 5 (1987):139–148; Baron-Cohen, "The Development of a Theory of Mind in Autism: Deviance and Delay?
23. Baron-Cohen, "Are Autistic Children 'Behaviorists'?"
24. P. L. Harris and A. Muncer, "Autistic Children's Understanding of Beliefs and Desires" (Paper presented at the British Psychological Society Developmental Section Conference, Harlech, Wales, Sept. 1988).
25. P. L. Harris, *Children and Emotion: The Development of Psychological Understanding* (Oxford: Basil Blackwell, 1989), Chap. 9.
26. S. Baron-Cohen, "Do People with Autism Understand What Causes Emotion?" *Child Development* 62 (1991):385–395.
27. R. P. Hobson, "The Autistic Child's Appraisal of Expressions of Emotion," *Journal of Child Psychology and Psychiatry* 27 (1986):321–342; and "The Autistic Child's Appraisal of Expressions of Emotion: A Further Study," *Journal of Child Psychology and Psychiatry* 27 (1986):671–680.
28. R. P. Hobson, "Beyond Cognition: A Theory of Autism," in *Autism: New Perspectives on Diagnosis, Nature and Treatment,* ed. G. Dawson (New York: Guilford Press, 1989), pp. 22–48.
29. M. Sigman, P. Mundy, T. Sherman, and J. Ungerer, "Social Interactions of Autistic, Mentally Retarded, and Normal Children and Their Caregivers," *Journal of Child Psychology and Psychiatry* 27 (1986):647–656.
30. S. Baron-Cohen, "From Attention-goal Psychology to Belief–desire Psychology: The Development of a Theory of Mind, and its Dysfunction," in *Understanding Other Minds:*

Perspectives from Autism, ed. S. Baron-Cohen, H. Tager-Flusberg and D. Cohen (Oxford: Oxford University Press, 1993), pp. 59–82.

31. Leslie and Frith, "Autistic Children's Understanding of Seeing, Knowing and Believing"; Perner, Frith, Leslie, and Leekam, "Exploration of the Autistic Child's Theory of Mind."

32. A. M. Leslie, "The Theory of Mind Impairment in Autism: Evidence for a Modular Mechanism of Development?" in *Natural Theories of Mind: Evolution, Development and Simulation of Everyday Mindreading,* ed. A. Whiten (Oxford: Basil Blackwell, 1991), pp. 63–78.

33. Frith, *Autism.*

34. Ibid., pp. 118–119.

35. S. Baron-Cohen, "Precursors to a Theory of Mind: Understanding Attention in Others," in *Natural Theories of Mind: Evolution, Development and Simulation of Everyday Mindreading,* ed. A. Whiten (Oxford: Basil Blackwell, 1991), pp. 232–251.

36. Baron-Cohen, "From Attention-goal Psychology to Belief-desire Psychology."

37. S. Baron-Cohen, J. Allen, and C. Gillberg, "Can Autism Be Detected at 18 Months? The Needle, the Haystack, and the CHAT," *British Journal of Psychiatry* 161 (1992):839–843.

38. I. Bretherton, S. McNew, and M. Beeghly-Smith, "Early Person Knowledge as Expressed in Gestural and Verbal Communication: When Do Infants Acquire a 'Theory of Mind'?" in *Infant Social Cognition,* ed. M. E. Lamb and L. R. Sherod (Hillsdale, N.J.: Erlbaum, 1981), pp. 333–373.

39. S. Baron-Cohen, "The Autistic Child's Theory of Mind: A Case of Specific Developmental Delay," *Journal of Child Psychology and Psychiatry* 30 (1989):285–297.

40. F. G. E. Happé, "A Test of Relevance Theory: Communicative Competence and Theory of Mind in Autism" *Cognition* (in press).

41. F. G. E. Happé, "An Advanced Test of Theory of Mind: Understanding of Story Characters' Thoughts and Feelings by Able Autistic, Mentally Handicapped and Normal

Children and Adults" *Journal of Autism and Developmental Disorders* (in press).

42. D. Sperber and D. Wilson, *Relevance: Communication and Cognition* (Cambridge, Mass.: Harvard University Press, 1986).

43. Park, *The Siege,* p. 325.

44. Ibid., p. 287.

45. Ibid., p. 290.

10 / CAUSES AND CONSEQUENCES

1. S. Carey, "On Some Relations between the Description and the Explanation of Developmental Change," in *Causes of Development,* ed. G. Butterworth and P. Bryant (London: Harvester Wheatsheaf, 1990), pp. 135–157.

2. D. R. Olson, "Making up Your Mind," Presidential address to the Canadian Psychological Association, June 1989, *Canadian Psychology* 30 (1989):617–627.

3. B. Snell, *The Discovery of the Mind in Greek Philosophy and Literature* (New York: Dover, 1982. Originally published in German in 1948).

4. C. F. Feldman, "The New Theory of Theory of Mind," *Human Development* 35 (1992):107–117.

5. J. S. Bruner, "The Growth of Mind," Presidential address to the American Psychological Association, Sept. 1965, *American Psychologist* 20 (1965):1007–1017.

6. J. Bruner, *Acts of Meaning* (Cambridge, Mass.: Harvard University Press, 1990).

7. J. Dunn, *The Beginnings of Social Understanding* (Cambridge, Mass.: Harvard University Press, 1988).

8. Ibid., p. 57.

9. B. B. Scheiffelin and E. Ochs, *Language Socialization across Cultures* (Cambridge: Cambridge University Press, 1986).

10. J. Avis and P. L. Harris, "Belief-desire Reasoning among Baka Children: Evidence for a Universal Conception of Mind," *Child Development* 62 (1991):460–467.

11. A. Whiten, (ed.), *Natural Theories of Mind: Evolution, Devel-*

opment and Simulation of Everyday Mindreading (Oxford: Basil Blackwell, 1991).

12. A. M. Leslie, "The Theory of Mind Impairment in Autism: Evidence for a Modular Mechanism of Development?" in *Natural Theories of Mind*, ed. A. Whiten, pp. 63–78.

13. P. L. Harris, "The Work of the Imagination," in *Natural Theories of Mind*, ed. A. Whiten, pp. 283–304.

14. C. N. Johnson, "Theory of Mind and the Structure of Conscious Experience," in *Developing Theories of Mind*, ed. J. W. Astington, P. L. Harris, and D. R. Olson (New York: Cambridge University Press, 1988), pp. 47–63.

15. P. L. Harris, "From Simulation to Folk Psychology: The Case for Development," *Mind & Language* 7 (1992):120–144.

16. J. Perner and D. Howes, "'He Thinks he Knows'; and More Developmental Evidence against the Simulation (Role Taking) Theory," *Mind & Language* 7 (1992):72–86; J. H. Flavell, P. T. Botkin, C. L. Fry, J. W. Wright, and P. E. Jarvis, *The Development of Role-taking and Communication Skills in Children* (New York: Wiley, 1968).

17. S. Carey, *Conceptual Change in Childhood* (Cambridge, Mass.: Bradford/MIT Press, 1985); A. Karmiloff-Smith, "The Child is a Theoretician Not an Inductivist," *Mind & Language* 3 (1988):183–197; F. C. Keil, *Concepts, Kinds, and Cognitive Development* (Cambridge, Mass.: Bradford/MIT Press, 1989).

18. J. Russell, "The Theory-theory: So Good They Named It Twice?" *Cognitive Development* 7 (1992):485–519. It is only fair to point out that Russell himself does not think the Theory view is so good at all.

19. A. Gopnik and H. M. Wellman, "The Theory Theory," in *Domain Specificity in Cognition and Culture*, ed. L. Hirschfeld and S. Gelman (New York: Cambridge University Press, in press).

20. J. Perner, *Understanding the Representational Mind* (Cambridge, Mass.: Bradford Books/MIT Press, 1991).

21. J. W. Astington and A. Gopnik, "Developing Understanding of Desire and Intention," in *Natural Theories of Mind*, ed. Whiten, pp. 39–50.

22. Gopnik and Wellman, "The Theory Theory."
23. K. Bartsch and H. M. Wellman, "Young Children's Attribution of Action to Beliefs and Desires," *Child Development* 60 (1989):946–964.
24. R. Case, "A Neo-Piagetian Analysis of the Child's Understanding of Other People, and the Internal Conditions which Motivate Their Behavior" (Paper presented at the Biennial Meeting of the Society for Research in Child Development, Kansas City, Mo., April 1989).
25. D. Frye, P. D. Zelazo, and T. Palfai, "The Cognitive Basis of Theory of Mind" (Unpublished manuscript, New York University, 1992).
26. D. R. Olson, "The Development of Representations: The Origins of Mental Life," *Canadian Psychology* 34 (1993): 293–306.
27. A. Gopnik and V. Slaughter, "Young Children's Understanding of Changes in Their Mental States," *Child Development* 62 (1991):98–110.
28. J. Perner, T. Ruffman, and S. Leekam, "Theory of Mind Is Contagious: You Catch It from Your Sibs," *Child Development* (in press).
29. P. Bryant, "Empirical Evidence for Causes in Development," in *Causes of Development*, ed. G. Butterworth and P. Bryant (London: Harvester Wheatsheaf, 1990), pp. 33–45.
30. J. Dunn, J. Brown, C. Slomkowski, C. Tesla, and L. Youngblade, "Young Children's Understanding of Other People's Feelings and Beliefs: Individual Differences and Their Antecedents," *Child Development* 62 (1991):1352–1366.
31. J. M. Jenkins and J. W. Astington, "Cognitive, Linguistic, and Social Factors Associated with Theory of Mind Development in Young Children" (Paper presented at the Biennial Meeting of the Society for Research in Child Development, New Orleans, March 1993).
32. M. Tomasello, A. Kruger, and H. H. Ratner, "Cultural Learning," *Behavioral and Brain Sciences* (in press).
33. H. Gardner, *The Unschooled Mind* (New York: Basic Books, 1991).
34. M. Rutter and L. Bartak, "Special Education Treatment of

Autistic Children: A Comparative Study, II: Follow-up Findings and Implications for Services," *Journal of Child Psychology and Psychiatry* 14 (1973):241–270.

35. V. G. Paley, *Wally's Stories* (Cambridge, Mass.: Harvard University Press, 1981), p. 216.

36. V. G. Paley, *Boys and Girls: Superheroes in the Doll Corner* (Chicago: University of Chicago Press, 1984), p. 59.

37. Paley, *Wally's Stories,* pp. 183–184.

38. Ibid., p. 140.

39. C. Moore, D. Furrow, L. Chiasson, and M. Patriquin, "Developmental Relationships between Production and Comprehension of Mental Terms" *First Language* (in press).

40. M. P. Robinson, "Children's Understanding of the Distinction between Messages and Meanings: Emergence and Implications," in *Children of Social Worlds,* ed. M. Richards and P. Light (Oxford: Polity Press/Blackwells, 1986), pp. 213–232.

41. G. Wells, *Language Development in the Pre-school Years* (Cambridge: Cambridge University Press, 1985).

42. This incident was observed by one of my students, Jacqueline Richman.

43. M. Donaldson, *Children's Minds* (Glasgow: Fontana/Collins, 1978).

44. Ibid., pp. 88–89.

45. L. S. Vygotsky, *Thought and Language* (Cambridge, Mass.: MIT Press, 1962. Originally published in Russian in 1934), pp. 91, 92.

Suggested Reading

J. W. Astington, P. L. Harris, and D. R. Olson, eds. *Developing Theories of Mind.* New York: Cambridge University Press, 1988.

S. Baron-Cohen, H. Tager-Flusberg and D. Cohen, eds. *Understanding Other Minds: Perspectives from Autism.* Oxford: Oxford University Press, 1993.

G. E. Butterworth, P. L. Harris, A. M. Leslie, and H. M. Wellman, eds. *Perspectives on the Child's Theory of Mind.* Oxford: Oxford University Press, 1991.

J. Dunn. *The Beginnings of Social Understanding.* Cambridge, Mass.: Harvard University Press, 1988.

U. Frith *Autism: Explaining the Enigma.* Oxford: Basil Blackwell, 1989.

D. Frye and C. Moore, eds. *Children's Theories of Mind: Mental States and Social Understanding.* Hillsdale, N.J.: Erlbaum, 1991.

P. L. Harris. *Children and Emotion: The Development of Psychological Understanding.* Oxford: Basil Blackwell, 1989.

J. Perner. *Understanding the Representational Mind.* Cambridge, Mass.: Bradford/MIT Press, 1991.

H. M. Wellman. *The Child's Theory of Mind.* Cambridge, Mass.: Bradford/MIT Press, 1990.

A. Whiten, ed. *Natural Theories of Mind: Evolution, Development and Simulation of Everyday Mindreading.* Oxford: Basil Blackwell, 1991.

Index